PEARLS

FOR THE SHABBOS TABLE

From the teachings of
THE LUBAVITCHER REBBE
Rabbi Menachem M. Schneerson
זצוקללה"ה נבג"מ זי"ע

ADAPTED BY
RABBI YOSEF Y. ALPEROWITZ

Published by
KEHOT PUBLICATION SOCIETY
770 Eastern Parkway, Brooklyn, NY 11213
5769 • 2009

PEARLS FOR THE SHABBOS TABLE

Published and Copyrighted © 2009
by
KEHOT PUBLICATION SOCIETY
770 Eastern Parkway / Brooklyn, New York 11213
(718) 774-4000 / Fax (718) 774-2718
editor@kehot.com

Orders:
291 Kingston Avenue / Brooklyn, New York 11213
(718) 778-0226 / Fax (718) 778-4148
www.kehot.com

ISBN: 978-0-8266-0096-7

Printed in Canada

PEARLS FOR THE
SHABBOS
TABLE

CONTENTS

BOOK OF VAYIKRA

INTRODUCTION

With thanks to the Almighty, it is my pleasure to present *Pearls for the Shabbos Table*.

The Torah tells us that "Hashem blessed the Seventh day and He made it holy."[1] This means that the day of Shabbos is not just a day of rest, but also a day of spiritual elevation and holiness.

One of the ways of experiencing this is by sharing a *D'var Torah* at the Shabbos table.

For many years, on Shabbos afternoons, the Lubavitcher Rebbe, Rabbi Menachem M. Schneerson ז"יע, conducted a *farbrengen* (communal gathering) in which he delivered brilliant Torah discourses. For hours upon hours, the thousands who attended literally entered into a world of elevation and holiness—the true spirit of *Shabbos Kodesh*.

Throughout the years of his leadership, the Rebbe delivered public addresses for more than 11,000 hours. When translated into English and completely published, the Rebbe's vast Torah teachings will fill hundreds of volumes.

Present at the Rebbe's *farbrengens* were men, women, children, the scholar and the layman—all united as one. As a true leader of the Jewish people, the Rebbe had the ability

1. *Bereishis* 2:3.

to unite all the segments of our people and truthfully, his messages are, as they were, applicable to all the people of Israel.

Whilst no attempt is made in this book to provide a translation of any of the Rebbe's complete talks, it is my hope, that it will help recapture a tiny fraction of the splendour of the Rebbe's talks for every man, woman and child, at the Shabbos Table. Its simple style will help beginners become familiar with many concepts that are explained at greater length and depth in the Rebbe's original talks. At the same time, its powerful messages will nourish the minds and the souls of the more seasoned scholars.[2]

Its date of publication, by Divine Providence, significantly underscores the above. The year 5769 is a Year of *Hakhel*, when all the people of Israel, men, women and children gathered to the *Beis Hamikdosh* to listen to the King read from the Torah.

Indeed, the contents of this book have already inspired men, women and children. Originally prepared for two children that I had the privilege to tutor privately a few years ago, the children—to whom this book is dedicated—have inspired their parents and their guests, as they shared these "pearls" at the Shabbos table.

---

2. However, in no way can this book substitute studying the original talks of the Rebbe which are absolutely vital for full comprehension of the subject matter. The sources have thus been provided.

Ideal for every Jewish home, for parents, for children, for teachers and private tutors—this book will enable countless others to experience the same pleasure and joy.

I would gratefully like to acknowledge and thank Rabbis Yosef B. Friedman, Dovid Olidort, Avraham D. Vaisfiche, Yirmi Berkowitz and Mendel Laine for carefully reviewing, editing and preparing the book for publication. I would also like to give special thanks to my wife Chana, for her support and encouragement through the entire project. It is my hope and prayer that we should be blessed with abundant success in fulfilling the Rebbe's Shlichus in Bournemouth, with true *nachas* from our dear children, continuing to raise them as proud soldiers in the family of Shluchim worldwide.

The Rebbe explains, that it is the duty of every Chassid to be a "lamplighter", i.e. to help each Jew discover his inner soul—which is compared to a flame—and to help every Jew ignite the spark of that soul, through the flame of mitzvos, until it shines brightly.

As this book goes to print, we mourn for our colleagues Rabbi Gavriel & Rivkah Holtzberg, the Shluchim to Mumbai, India, and for all those who were brutally murdered at the Chabad Center in Mumbai, may G-d avenge their blood. These Shluchim were selflessly devoted to actualizing the Rebbe's vision of reaching every Jew, and while they were truly great light "lamplighters" at any time, it was, of course, at their Shabbos Table where they "kindled" more souls of men, women and children than ever.

May the Rebbe's teachings in this book continue to "kindle" the souls of men, women, and children at many Shabbos Tables throughout the world—thus keeping their legacy alive and bring comfort to their families, to the family of the Shluchim, and to all of Israel.

May these teachings illuminate many Jewish homes with the true light of Shabbos, and may this light dispel the darkness of exile, with the coming of Moshiach, when we will witness the ultimate *Hakhel*—the ingathering of all the exiles with eternal joy, to the Land of Israel and to the *Beis Hamikdosh*—speedily in our days.

RABBI YOSEF Y. ALPEROWITZ

14 Kislev 5769
Year of Hakhel
80th Wedding Anniversary of the Lubavitcher Rebbe,
Rabbi Menachem M. Schneerson, and Rebbetzin Chaya Mushka,
of righteous memory
Bournemouth, UK

ספר
בראשית

BOOK OF
BEREISHIS

בראשית
BEREISHIS

THE SHABBOS THAT SETS THE
COURSE FOR THE YEAR

The Torah begins with the verse: בְּרֵאשִׁית בָּרָא אֱלֹקִים אֵת הַשָּׁמַיִם וְאֵת הָאָרֶץ ("In the beginning of Hashem's creating the heavens and the earth"). The first word of the Torah is *Bereishis*.

Our Sages teach us that the word *Bereishis* means much more than "In the beginning." Within its letters one can discover the purpose of creation, the reason Hashem made us exist.

The numeric value of the first letter of the word *Bereishis*—*Beis*—is two. The rest of the word, *reishis*, comes from the root word *rosh*, which means head. *Bereishis* refers to the two "heads"—the Torah and the Jewish people. Just as a "head" leads the body, the Torah is the guide that leads the Jewish people, who, in turn, have the responsibility to be a guide to all nations of the world.

Every Jew—even a child—should know that in the eyes of Hashem, he or she is considered a "head," a leader to whom all nations on earth can look up as a living example. The way a Jewish child behaves is important not only for his or her own sake, but for the sake of the entire world.

When a Jew displays fear of Hashem (for example, when a man or boy wears a *kippah* and *tzitzis*, or when a woman or girl dresses as required by Torah law), it has a ripple effect on friends and neighbors, because they are reminded of the Creator of heaven and earth.

Similarly, in the blessing of שֶׁהַכֹּל נִהְיָה בִּדְבָרוֹ —"by whose word *all* things came to be" before drinking water (for instance), we thank Hashem not only for creating the water, but rather, for creating the *entire* world. Thereby, we convey the message that all of creation must behave in accordance with Hashem's wishes.

Hashem has given us the power to influence all of heaven and earth. By doing so, we bring the blessings of Hashem upon all of creation.

Shabbos Bereishis is not just the Shabbos when we read "the beginning" of the Torah. Rather, like a head which leads and directs the body, *Shabbos Bereishis* sets the course for the entire year. Meaning that the upcoming year is strongly influenced by our good resolutions made on this day.

*(Based on Likkutei Sichos, vol. 1 p. 1; vol. 21 p. 311
Sichos 13 Av 5739; 18 Tishrei 5750; 24 Kislev 5752)*

נח
NOACH

THE IMPORTANCE OF CARING FOR OTHERS

The *Zohar* discusses the difference between Noach and Moshe Rabbeinu. Moshe prayed to Hashem to spare the people in his generation (who sinned by worshiping the Golden Calf) from punishment. Moshe's prayers made a difference, and his people did not perish. Noach, on the other hand, did not pray to Hashem that the people of his generation should survive the flood, and they perished.

The *Zohar* mentions two opinions: One opinion excuses Noach for his conduct—maintaining that the reason why Noach did not act like Moshe is because Moshe "did not rely on his own merit, but on that of Avraham, Yitzchak, and Yaakov," which is something that Noach could not have done, of course. The second opinion maintains that nevertheless, Noach should have prayed for his generation.

We find a similar idea in the beginning of this week's *parshah*, where the Torah describes Noach as "a righteous man, faultless in his generations." Rashi explains this phrase by quoting two opinions: Some Sages say that the Torah is teaching us that Noach was very righteous even though most people in his generation were wicked, and that had he been alive in the time of other *tzaddikim*, he would have been even more righteous. Other Sages maintain that the Torah is teaching us that Noach was considered righteous only in comparison to the wicked people of *his* generation. But had he been alive in the generation of Avraham Avinu, he would not have been considered special.

In either argument, the first opinion clearly praises Noach: a) he was not to blame for his behavior b) had he lived in a generation of *tzaddikim* he would have been more righteous. The second opinion seems to be undermining his greatness.

But truthfully, even the second opinion acknowledges that Noach was a righteous man. Its main argument is only that the Torah—a book of lessons for every day and age— teaches us that it would be inappropriate for *us* to emulate Noach.

For in *his* generation, Noach did not have anyone to look up to, and, without the merit of Avraham, Yitzchak, and Yaakov, did not feel himself adequate enough to pray to Hashem. But we, the descendants of Avraham, Yitzchak, and Yaakov, must make every effort to pray to Hashem even on behalf of others whom we may consider to be "sinners," for these prayers can make a big difference.

(Based on Likkutei Sichos, vol. 25 p. 19)

pearls for the
shabbos table

לך לך
LECH LECHA

THE DIFFERENCE
BEFORE AND AFTER

This week's *parshah* relates the story of Avraham Avinu's life, beginning with Hashem commanding him to journey to Canaan, at the age of seventy-five.

Why is this the opening incident? After all, Avraham had already achieved great things and accomplished so much in his life, and indeed, the Midrash tells us that Avraham was three years old when he discovered Hashem. Ever since then, he taught, educated and influenced many people so that they recognized the one true G-d. For this, he was thrown into prison and sentenced to death in a fiery furnace, yet was miraculously saved. Many people were inspired by Avraham and his wife, Sarah, and tried to follow in their footsteps.

All this occured before Avraham was commanded to leave for Canaan. Yet the Torah does not relate any of these events. At the end of last week's *parshah* we read about Avraham's birth, marriage and journey to Charan in a few short verses. The next thing we know, Avraham is already seventy five years old!

Why are the details of his life up to this point unimportant?

Chasidus answers this question by explaining the difference between Avraham's life experiences before and after *Lech Lecha*.

Everything Avraham did up until this point was based on his own understanding. He figured out that the world could not exist without a Creator. It made sense. That's why he believed in Hashem. That's why he taught this to the world. He felt that his faith was a true faith and was even prepared to give his life for it.

Now, for the first time, Hashem appears to Avraham and challenges him to do something that did not make sense to him. He is told to move out and leave his home, with no explanation!

The story about the first Jew does not begin simply with Avraham's own discoveries or with his journey to Canaan, but rather with: "*Hashem* said to Avram, 'Go... to the land which *I* will show you.'"

Judaism is not based on human intellect (what we understand and feel), rather on our ability to do exactly what Hashem commands us to do, even when it is not understood.

Therefore the Torah doesn't elaborate on Avraham's past achievements, but instead focuses on his new, higher level of commitment to Hashem.

(Based on Likkutei Sichos, vol. 25 p. 47)

pearls for the
shabbos table

7

וירא
VAYEIRA

KINDNESS—
THE FOUNDATION OF JUDAISM

This week's *parshah* begins by telling us about Avraham and Sarah's incredible *hachnasas orchim* and generosity. Even while he was recovering after his *bris milah*, Avraham sat in the heat of the sun, awaiting passers-by to invite as guests. When he noticed three men in the distance, he ran towards them to welcome them. Avraham and Sarah gave them the best they could possibly offer. These guests were three angels disguised as men. One of them foretold that Avraham and Sarah would be blessed with a child the following year.

Towards the end of the *parshah*, we read about the birth of Yitzchak—Avraham and Sarah's only child—exactly one year later, as the angel had foretold.

The connection between these two events seems simple, for had they not welcomed the three guests they would not have received the news regarding Yitzchak's birth.

Another explanation:

Yitzchak was the first person in history to be born as a Jew. By recounting the hospitality and generosity of his parents before his birth, the Torah is teaching us how important these values are in Judaism.

We see that Avraham's and Sarah's hospitality and *gemilus chasadim* led to the birth of the Jewish people.

Avraham and Sarah taught their son Yitzchak to follow in their ways, and to pass this on to his children and all generations to come, as it is written in this week's *parshah*: "He instructs his sons and his household after him to keep the way of Hashem, practicing *tzedakah* and justice."

Thus we learn that *tzedakah* and *chesed* are among the most essential matters in the lives of every single Jew.

(Based on Sichas 19 Nissan 5741)

חיי שרה
CHAYEI SARA

RIVKAH AND THE
THREE MITZVOS OF WOMEN

I n this week's *parshah*, we read about the marriage of Yitzchak and Rivkah.

The Midrash tells us that Yitzchak wanted to determine how righteous and holy Rivkah was.

How would he be able to tell?

Rashi writes that during Sarah's life, three special miracles happened in her merit: 1) Her Shabbos candles remained kindled all week long, until it was time to light them again. 2) The challah she baked remained fresh all week long. 3) A special cloud hovered above her tent.

When Rivkah entered Yitzchak's home, he noticed that these miracles, which had not occurred since Sarah's passing, resumed once again. Seeing that Rivkah was righteous like Sarah, he knew that she deserved to be a Matriarch of the Jewish people.

Why did the Matriarchs merit these miracles?

These three miracles symbolize the three *mitzvos* that Jewish women are responsible for. The first—lighting

Shabbos candles; the second—separating Challah (and keeping a kosher home); the third—family purity (and maintaining the sanctity and holiness of those inside the home).

Reversing the order of these miracles from the sequential order originally described in Midrash, Rashi mentions the miracle of the Shabbos candles as the *first* miracle. For this miracle—which occured in connection with a mitzvah that she did—emphasizes *Rivkah's* greatness and righteousness.

According to the Midrash, Rivkah was only three years old at that time!

This is a lesson for every Jewish woman and girl—including little three year old girls: Every daughter of Israel is considered *bas* Sarah, Rivkah, Rachel and Leah. Through lighting the Shabbos candles, she has the power to illuminate her home and to transform it into a home of blessing, purity and holiness all week long.

(Based on Likkutei Sichos, vol. 15 p. 171)

תולדות
TOLDOS

THE DAILY BIRTH
OF THE SOUL

R osh Chodesh Kislev always occurs during the week of, or is blessed on, Shabbos *parshas Toldos*. Surely there is a connection between the two.

Toldos recounts the birth of Yitzchak and Rivkah's children, Yaakov and Esav. Its name, *Toldos*, is related to *leida*, meaning "birth."

Every newborn child is carried by its mother for nine months prior to being born. During this time, the child is hidden. The child is revealed only upon birth.

Similarly, the start of every Jewish month—*Rosh Chodesh*—is like a "birth," as it takes place when the "birth" (*molad*) of the new moon occurs: The moon shines at all times, even when it is invisible. At the end of every Jewish month, the moon reaches a point where its light cannot be seen on Earth. *Rosh Chodesh* is the day when the moon reaches a point where its light becomes visible to us once again.

The name of this month—Kislev—alludes to this idea of concealment and revelation. The word כִּסְלֵו consists of two parts. The first part is: כִּס (*kis*)—from כִּיסוּי (*kisui*) or כִּסָּה (*kisah*) (*keseh*), meaning "covering" or "concealment." The second part consists of the letters לִ (*lamed vav*)—numerically equal to אֵלֶּה (*eileh*), which means "these are"—a term that describes the visible—and thus indicates "revelation."

We can apply this concept to our daily lives:

The *neshamah* exists within us at all times; even when we sleep at night our *neshamah* is there, but it is "hidden." As soon as we awaken, the *neshamah* becomes revealed. Thus, upon awakening, we immediately thank Hashem for allowing our *neshamah* to be revealed again, by reciting *Modeh ani lefanecha melech chai vekayam shehechezarta bi nishmasi* ("I offer thanks to You, living and eternal King, for You have restored my soul within me").

In the Hebrew, the very first word of the day is *Modeh* (thanks)—one says *Modeh* even before *ani* (I), placing Hashem before one's self. This expression of thanks stems from the essence of the soul, which is always bound to the essence of Hashem.

(Based on Sefer Hasichos 5752 p. 120-128)

ויצא
VAYEITZEI

PRAYER—THE LADDER THAT CONNECTS US TO HASHEM

This Shabbos we read the story of Yaakov's journey to Charan. The Torah tells us that during his travels, it became dark, and Yaakov stopped to pray. Feeling tired, Yaakov lay down to rest. Soon after, he had a dream in which he saw a ladder that was standing on the ground and reached all the way up to Heaven. Angels from Heaven were ascending and descending it.

We know that the stories told in the Torah are not merely events that have transpired, and that the Torah relates these stories to us because *maaseh avos siman lebanim*— the stories of our Patriarchs are a "sign" (a lesson) for their children, for every Jew, in every day and age.

Indeed, Yaakov's dream was a "vision" of the future of the Jewish people.

Usually, a ladder is used to help us reach something beyond our normal reach. The Jewish people have a "ladder" through which we can reach Heaven: the "ladder" of *tefillah*. Much like the ladder in Yaakov's dream, we stand with our feet on the earth when we pray, yet our minds and our hearts reach the highest heavens. This is how ordinary human beings are able to speak to Hashem.

Just as ladders have a number of steps, so do our daily morning prayers:

Step one—acknowledging Hashem (beginning with *Modeh Ani* and *Hodu*).

Step two—praising Hashem (in the *Pesukei Dezimrah*— "Verses of Praise").

Step three—loving Hashem (in the *Shema*—"You shall love Hashem").

Step four—serving Hashem (in the *Amidah*—when we stand as servants before our Master).

As we pray, some angels ascend the "ladder" to Heaven to bring our requests before Hashem, while other angels descend and bring Hashem's answers to us.

(Based on Hayom Yom 5 Kislev; Likkutei Sichos, vol. 1 p. 200;
vol. 24 p. 646; Sefer Hamaamorim 5722 p. 92;
Toras Menachem—Sefer Hamaamorim Melukot, vol. 2 p. 54;
See also above, p. 13)

וישלח
VAYISHLACH

CHOOSING OUR PRIORITIES

In the beginning of this week's *parshah*, we read that Yaakov sent a message to Esav in which he said: עִם לָבָן גַּרְתִּי ("I lived with Lavan").

Rashi explains that the word גַּרְתִּי (*garti*) comes from the word גֵּר (*geir*), which means a stranger. In other words, Yaakov told Esav that there was no need for him to be jealous of the blessings Yaakov had received from Yitzchak, because the blessings were never fulfilled. Thirty four years had passed since he had left home, and most of these years he had lived like a "stranger."

Rashi then offers another interpretation of the word *garti*: The *gematria* of גַּרְתִּי is 613, alluding to the 613 *mitzvos*. According to this explanation, Yaakov was telling Esav that in all the years he stayed in Lavan's home, he kept the 613 commandments.

On a deeper level, these two explanations of the word *garti* are connected:

Yaakov continued telling Esav that he now owned many animals and servants. Nevertheless, Yaakov considered all this material wealth as something that was "foreign" to him. What mattered to him were the needs of his soul, i.e. Torah and *mitzvos*.

This idea is also indicated later on in the *parshah*, where the Torah tells us that "Yaakov built for himself a home, and for his cattle he made huts."

One difference between a "home" and a "hut" is that at home—where one usually lives—everything is important, but in a "hut"—which one enters only temporarily—the details are not as significant. Yaakov's "home" alludes to his spiritual matters, which was most important to him. But for his material belongings, he merely made huts.

That's why Yaakov said: "*im lavan garti*," I regarded all the material matters that I earned in Lavan's home like a stranger, and therefore, I always managed to keep all the 613 commandments of the Torah.

The lesson from this is as follows:

Looking at the world around us, it is not so easy to be a Jew. Wherever we turn, there are many modern "Esavs" who hate us and many modern "Lavans" who wish to separate us from our Jewish roots.

The Torah is teaching us that there is only one way to overcome them: We must learn from Yaakov how to choose our priorities.

As Jews, we must always know that we were not sent in to this world just to eat, drink and sleep. In all these matters, we are like "strangers"—they are foreign to us. Yes, these are required. However, our real purpose on earth is to keep Hashem's 613 commandments. That is the most important thing in our lives.

(Based on Likkutei Sichos, vol. 1 p. 68)

OUT OF DARKNESS COMES
A GREAT LIGHT

This week's *parshah* is called *Vayeishev*—which means "He (Yaakov) dwelled" (literally, "He sat").

Rashi explains that this expression alludes to the peaceful, "settled" life which Yaakov was hoping for, but did not always have. First he suffered from Esav and from Lavan. Then, his daughter Dinah was captured, and finally he had the trouble with Yosef and his brothers.

This *parshah* deals with the story of Yosef. Ultimately (as we will read in a few weeks time), Yosef brought Yaakov to Egypt, where Yaakov's wish—to have a peaceful life—was finally granted. But in order for that to happen, Yosef was first hated and sold by his brothers to non-Jews, who took him to Egypt, where he was thrown in prison.

We do not—and cannot—understand the ways of Hashem. We do not understand why, so many times, good people like Yaakov and Yosef have to suffer. But, as Yosef would later tell his brothers, it was all part of Hashem's plan.

Eventually, Yosef was released from prison, and was appointed to be viceroy of the entire country. As a result of this, he saved Yaakov, his family and all the people of the land from the famine.

Most years, *parshas* Vayeishev is read in the same week that we celebrate the 19th of Kislev, the day Rabbi Schneur Zalman of Liadi (the Alter Rebbe, first Rebbe of Chabad), was released from prison in 5559 (1798).

Throughout his life, the Alter Rebbe suffered in the same way that Yosef did. He, too, was envied by some of his "brothers" (fellow Jews), "sold" to non-Jews and thrown in prison on false charges. But as a result of all these hardships, the Alter Rebbe's righteousness became known. After his release, more and more people became attracted to his teachings. Indeed, these teachings have since expanded, and throughout the subsequent generations have saved countless Jewish souls, returning them to their heritage and preparing the world for the coming of Moshiach.

(Based on Likkutei Sichos, vol. 25 p. 193)

מקץ
MIKEITZ

WHY REUVEN POURS SALT
ON THE WOUND

In this week's *parshah*, the Torah tells us that when Shimon was imprisoned, Yosef's brothers expressed regret for what they had done to Yosef. They said to each other, "we are having this trouble now because of the way we once treated Yosef." Hearing this, Reuven, the eldest son, replied: "I told you not to sin against the child!"

As we know from the previous Torah portion, Reuven knew all along that his brothers were wrong. That's why he originally intended to save Yosef from his brothers. He was unable to do so, however, because he was not present when Yosef was sold, as he was at home attending to Yaakov at that time.

The brothers had clearly realized that they were wrong. They had admitted their guilt, and were already heartbroken. Why, then, did Reuven say: "I *told* you"?

The truth is that Reuven was teaching his brothers the true meaning of *teshuvah*. He heard his brothers say that they were sorry for what they did to Yosef because of the troubles they were now going through. But Reuven wished to teach them that being sorry means to regret what is wrong because it is wrong, *because it is a sin*, and not because one gets in trouble.

As the Rambam explains, true *teshuvah* means that you have reached the point that Hashem can testify that you will not commit the sin again. But if one expresses remorse only because one is in trouble, who knows what will happen when the trouble passes?

This is why Reuven had to tell them, "I told you not to sin": You must remember that the problem is that you sinned, not that you are being punished. Only when one regrets the sin itself can there be true *teshuvah*.

(Based on Likkutei Sichos, vol. 30 p. 198)

חנוכה
CHANUKAH

FOCUSING ON THE EDUCATION
OF OUR CHILDREN

Chanukah is a festival that celebrates the miracle of the recapture and rededication of the *Beis Hamikdosh* by a family of righteous *Kohanim*—the Chashmonaim.

The word חֲנוּכָּה itself reminds us of the story of Chanukah. It stands for two words חָנוּ ("they—the Chashmonaim—rested" from the war they had fought), and כה (which equals 25, referring to the 25th day of the month of Kislev, which is when Chanukah is observed).

Chanukah also means dedication or consecration (as in a *chanukas habayis*). This is because after gaining entry to the *Beis Hamikdosh*, the *Kohanim* cleansed it and restored the daily services. In that sense, a consecration of the *Beis Hamikdosh* actually took place on Chanukah.

The word חֲנוּכָּה is also related to the word חִנוּךְ (*chinuch*), which means "education."

The lesson we can learn from all of the above is that Chanukah is a time to focus on the Jewish educational needs of our children. We should provide them with a holy environment—similar to a *Beis Hamikdosh*, purified and sanctified by the Chashmonaim—which will help them become true G-d-serving Jews.

Another lesson to be learned from Chanukah:

When the Chashmonaim entered the *Beis Hamikdosh*, they found only one jug of pure olive oil bearing the seal of the *Kohen Godol*, with which they kindled the *Menorah*. A miracle occurred and the oil—which contained only one day's supply—lasted for eight days, until they were able to produce new oil.

According to Jewish law, under these circumstances, the Chashmonaim were permitted to light the *Menorah* with impure oil. However, they did not want to compromise their observance of *mitzvos*. They would accept nothing but the best and they wanted a *Beis Hamikdosh* that was pure.

Similarly, we must offer our children an education of complete, uncompromised Judaism.

As an incentive for the children, it is therefore customary to give them money (*Chanukah gelt*) or gifts on Chanukah. These gifts should be given throughout Chanukah (except for Shabbos).

*(Based on Likkutei Sichos, vol. 1 p. 81;
Sefer Hasichos 5750, vol. 1. p. 194)*

וַיִּגַּשׁ
VAYIGASH

YOSEF REMAINS
SPIRITUALLY ALIVE IN EGYPT

I n this week's *parshah*, we read that when Yosef sent his
brothers back home to bring Yaakov to Egypt, he sent
them wagons that were loaded with many gifts. The Torah
tells us that when Yaakov first heard the news that Yosef
was alive, he didn't believe it. But when he saw the wagons,
his spirit suddenly became alive.

We can understand why Yaakov would be shocked to hear
that Yosef is alive. But why did he get so excited just from
seeing the wagons?

We are told that Yosef sent the wagons because the
Hebrew word for "wagons"—עֲגָלוֹת—is related to the word
עֶגְלָה, which means a "calf." The last thing Yaakov had
taught Yosef before Yosef left home, was the law of the
עֶגְלָה עֲרוּפָה—the axed calf (see *Devarim* 21:1-9). Yosef wanted to show his father that even after living twenty-two
years in Egypt, he still remembered the Torah they had
learned together.

Truthfully, Yaakov suspected all along that Yosef was alive.
He knew that Yosef's dreams were visions of the future,
which would one day come true, as Rashi explains in the

beginning of *Vayeishev*. However, Yaakov did not believe that Yosef was *spiritually* alive. To be a practicing Jew in a place like Egypt was unimaginable!

Yosef understood this, and that is precisely why he sent the wagons, to show his father that he had not forgotten his Torah education, and remained spiritually pure.

We can also see how well we ought to concentrate on our Torah studies. Yosef did not forget what he had learned even after twenty-two years had passed! We, too, must try *never* to forget the Torah that we learn.

(Based on Likkutei Sichos, vol. 10 p. 161; Sichas Zos Chanukah 5745)

וירחי
VAYECHI

HOW YAAKOV LIVED HIS
BEST YEARS IN EGYPT

This week's *parshah* begins with the *pasuk*: וַיְחִי יַעֲקֹב בְּאֶרֶץ מִצְרַיִם שְׁבַע עֶשְׂרֵה שָׁנָה ("Yaakov lived in the land of Egypt for seventeen years").

When Rabbi Menachem Mendel of Lubavitch (the Tzemach Tzedek) was a young boy and learned this passage, his teacher explained it according to the commentary of the *Baal Haturim*: "Our father Yaakov lived his seventeen *best* years in Egypt." This explanation is hinted at in the fact that the *gematria* of טוֹב (good) is seventeen.

When the Tzemach Tzedek returned home from cheder he asked his grandfather, Rabbi Schneur Zalman of Liadi (the Alter Rebbe), this question: How can it be that our father Yaakov, who is the most "preferred" of the Patriarchs, should have as the best years of his life the seventeen years that he lived in Egypt, a land of corruption?

The Alter Rebbe answered: It is written (in last week's portion) וְאֶת יְהוּדָה שָׁלַח לְפָנָיו אֶל יוֹסֵף לְהוֹרֹת לְפָנָיו גֹּשְׁנָה ("Yaakov sent Yehudah ahead of him to Yosef *lehoros*—to direct him—to Goshen").

book of
bereishis

26

The word *lehoros* is related to the word *Torah* and literally means "to teach." As Rashi writes, quoting the Midrash, before Yaakov came to Egypt, he sent Yehudah ahead of him to establish a house of study, so there would be a place for the tribes to study Torah.

Where was this yeshivah located?—in Goshen.

What is the meaning of "Goshen?"

The word "Goshen" is related to the word *hagasha*, which means "coming closer" (as in *Vayigash*, the name of last week's *parshah*).

So לְהוֹרֹת לְפָנָיו גֹּשְׁנָה means, in a deeper sense, that when one studies Torah, one comes closer to Hashem, so that even in Egypt one can be alive (*"Vayechi"*), making those years the best of one's life.

(Based on Hayom Yom 18 Teves)

ספר

שמות

BOOK OF

SHEMOS

שמות
SHEMOS

HOW JEWS ARE
COMPARED TO STARS

The name of this week's *parshah*—as well as the name of the second book of the Torah—is *Shemos* (Names). This is because the names of the tribes are mentioned, once again, in the beginning of this week's *parshah*.

The names of the tribes have already been mentioned numerous times in *Sefer Bereishis*. Why are they mentioned here again?

Rashi explains that this repeated listing of the names teaches us how precious the Children of Israel are in the eyes of Hashem. In His eyes, they are compared to the stars, which he counts and calls by name time and time again.

How are the Children of Israel compared to stars?

The stars shine in the night sky. By their light, even a person who walks in the darkness of the night will not lose his or her way. The same is true of the Children of Israel. Every Jew, man or woman, possesses enough moral and spiritual light to influence friends and acquaintances and guide them to the proper path.

But as we see in Rashi's explanation, Hashem *counts* and

names the stars. For there are two aspects to stars: a) every star is counted as a star, and all stars have that in common; b) each star is different, has a unique purpose and its own name. So, too, each and every one of the Children of Israel—equally—counts as a Jew. At the same time every individual has his or her own special quality and importance.

Another lesson from the stars:

Despite the great distance between us and the stars, we are able to see them and benefit from their light.

If we utilize the strength Hashem gave us, we have the ability—like stars—to illuminate not merely our immediate environment, but the entire world! Every single deed is important. Even one action, one word, or one thought of one *individual* can influence the *entire* world!

As the *Rambam* says, one should always consider that he and the entire world are being judged by Hashem for all their deeds, and the scales of justice are exactly even. One mitzvah can tip the scale to the side of merit and bring redemption to the entire world!

(Based on Hayom Yom 5 Cheshvan; Likkutei Sichos, vol. 6 p. 7; Toras Menachem 5742, vol. 3 p. 1192)

וארא
VA'EIRA

WHY MOSHE AND AARON
WERE CONSIDERED EQUAL

In this week's *parshah*, we read how Moshe and Aaron were instructed by Hashem to take the Children of Israel out of Egypt.

In one *pasuk* (6:26), the Torah mentions Aaron by name before Moshe, and one *pasuk* later (6:27), Moshe is mentioned before Aaron.

Why?

Rashi explains that the reason for this is to teach us that Moshe and Aaron were considered equally important.

In this week's *parshah* we also learn the reason why Hashem wanted to take the Children of Israel out of Egypt. This was so that he could make them His people.

This actually took place later, at Mt. Sinai, when Hashem gave us the Torah, an act referred to as Hashem's "marriage" to the Jewish people.

At every marriage, there are people who bring the groom to the *chuppah*, and those who bring the bride to the *chuppah*.

In this marriage between Hashem and the Jewish people at Mt. Sinai, there were also these two tasks. Here comes the equal functions of Moshe and Aaron: Moshe's task was to bring the Groom (Hashem) to the bride (the Jewish people). So he ascended Mt. Sinai so that he could bring Hashem to the people. And it was he who would bring the word of Hashem, the Torah, to the people.

Aaron's task was to encourage the bride to come closer to the Groom. So he remained with the people, befriending them and inspiring them to follow the Torah.

And each of these tasks was equally important.

(Based on Maamar Hu Aaron uMoshe, 5744)

בא
BO

WHY B'NEI YISRAEL
ARE CALLED TZIVOS HASHEM

In this week's *parshah* we read: וַיְהִי בְּעֶצֶם הַיּוֹם הַזֶּה יָצְאוּ כָּל צִבְאוֹת ה' מֵאֶרֶץ מִצְרָיִם ("On that day all the legions of Hashem went out of Egypt"). It is here that the Torah calls the people of Israel, *Tzivos Hashem*.

Tzivos is plural for *Tzava*. *Tzava* has three different meanings: a) an army; b) beauty; c) an amount of time.

As soon as Hashem took the people of Israel out of Egypt, He called them *Tzivos Hashem* for all three reasons:

a) They became part of Hashem's Army. Rule number one in an army is to follow instructions, no matter what. In the same way, Hashem has given us many *mitzvos*, and we must keep them, even if we don't understand them all.

b) Every individual was created with a specific character. Similarly, every single Jew is considered beautiful and important to Hashem. Each one has a special purpose in life that only he or she can accomplish. It does not suffice that "everyone else" will do it. Each person must fulfill the *mitzvos* for him or her self. The "beauty" of the Jewish people as a whole depends on each individual, just as a painting would be incomplete if it was lacking one specific color.

c) Hashem gives each person only a limited amount of time in which to accomplish his or her mission. Therefore, we must never push off an opportunity to do a mitzvah, because one does not know if there will be another chance. Every day and every moment given to us by Hashem is a blessing. We should cherish this G-d-given time and use it wisely.

*(Based on Maamar Hayosheves Baganim 5710,
Toras Menachem—Sefer Hamamarim Melukot, vol. 2 p. 405;
Sefer Hamamarim Basi Legani vol. 1 p. 129. See also above p. 31)*

בשלח
BESHALACH

THE NEED TO FIGHT AMALEK
IN EVERY GENERATION

This week's *parshah* concludes with the story of the battle with Amalek, a nation that waged war with the Children of Israel when they came out of Egypt. Hashem vowed to obliterate and fight Amalek in every generation.

The practical side of this concept bears little significance today, when we don't know who the nation of Amalek is. Its spiritual meaning, however, is as relevant today as ever.

Rashi compares Amalek's attack on the Jewish people to a hot bath into which no one could enter, until one person jumped in. While the man burned himself by doing so, he cooled off the bath for others. Likewise, until Amalek attacked, all nations feared the Jews. After hearing that Hashem miraculously took the Jews out of Egypt and punished the Egyptians when the Jews crossed the sea, no nation would dare fight them. By being first to attack the Jews, the nation of Amalek suffered, but now it became easier for other nations to attack.

The timing of their attack was also significant:

After leaving Egypt, the Jews entered the desert, where

Hashem gave them food from heaven and protected them from all the dangerous elements with the clouds of Glory. Amalek only attacked after the Jewish people expressed some doubts in their faith. The *gematria* of *Amalek* (עֲמָלֵק: 70+40+30+100=240) is the same as the *gematria* of *safek* (סָפֵק: 60+80+100=240), which means doubt.

Even though we are unable to identify the nation of Amalek, the concept of Amalek exists right within our own midst to this very day.

Amalek is represented by our *Yetzer Hara*, which casts doubts in our minds and attempts to cool us off from our excitement in all matters of our *Yiddishkeit*. We must therefore constantly fight against the influence of Amalek in our own lives, and our study of Torah and observance of *mitzvos* should be permeated with enthusiasm and fervor.

(Based on Likkutei Sichos, vol. 1 p. 146; vol. 2 p. 388)

טו בשבט
TU BISHVAT

MAN IS THE TREE OF THE FIELD

On Tu Bishvat (the fifteenth day of the month of Shevat), we celebrate the New Year for trees. At this time of the year, fresh sap rises from the soil, through the trunks of the trees, causing their continued growth. This day is relevant to every Jew, for the Torah tells us (*Devarim* 20:19) "Man is the tree of the field," and Hashem calls all the people of Israel (*Yeshayah* 60:21), "the branch of My planting."

It is customary to eat fruit of the trees on this day, and particularly fruit from the "seven kinds" of the Land of Israel. One of the many lessons we learn from this custom is that every Jew, like a tree, needs to grow in his or her *Yiddishkeit*. We must aspire to be like the "fruit" of the land that the Torah praises.

Furthermore, fruits contain seeds, which are usually small and seemingly insignificant. However, even the minutest details of these seeds—and the precise manner in which they are handled and planted—will reflect greatly in the trees that grow from these seeds later on.

Similarly, every little moment in the life of a child has a tremendous impact on the child's soul, even if its true value may only be fully appreciated in years to come.

Another lesson:

Even little seeds can be planted, and ultimately bear fruit. Similarly, Jewish children and students—even those young in age or with little knowledge—who are fortunate to receive a Jewish education themselves, have the power to "bear fruit" as well—to influence and inspire their fellow Jews to grow, like trees, in their Judaism.

(Based on Likkutei Sichos, vol. 6 p. 311;
Sichos 11 Shevat 5723 and 5727;
Toras Menachem 5742, vol. 2 p. 882)

יתרו
YISRO

BEING SENSITIVE TO
THE MIRACLES IN OUR LIVES

The theme of this week's *parshah* is *Matan Torah,* the Giving of the Torah.

In the beginning of the portion, we read about Yisro, Moshe Rabbeinu's father-in-law. He lived in a distant country, Midyan, where he was a priest among his people. Yet, when he heard of the miracles and wonders of *Yetzias Mitzrayim,* Yisro left his homeland and traveled out to the desert, to convert to Judaism and join the Jewish nation in accepting the Torah.

The Talmud (*Sotah* 11b) tells us that when the Jews left Egypt, the children were "the first to recognize Hashem." They acknowledged the miracles and wonders Hashem had performed even before their parents did, and certainly before Yisro had heard about them. Surely, the children were also aware that the purpose of *Yetzias Mitzrayim* was to receive the Torah from Hashem at Mt. Sinai.

This story serves as a lesson, especially for Jewish children:

If the miracles and wonders of *Yetzias Mitzrayim* had an

influence upon Yisro—to accept the Torah upon himself—certainly, they should have the same effect on Jewish children.

It is not too difficult to do so. We say in the blessing of *Modim* (in the *Amidah*), that there are constant miracles that Hashem performs for us. The awareness of these miracles should have an effect on our lives.

Every year, as the Shabbos of *Matan Torah* approaches, Jewish children should prepare themselves for the reading of the Ten Commandments, by firmly making up their minds to increase in all matters of Torah and *mitzvos*, and influence other children to do the same. They should do so with vigor and with joy.

(Based on Sichas 17 Shevat 5743)

משפטים
MISHPATIM

BEING CLEAR = BEING READY

This week's *parshah* opens with the verse: וְאֵלֶּה הַמִּשְׁפָּטִים אֲשֶׁר תָּשִׂים לִפְנֵיהֶם ("These are the laws which you shall set before them"). Rashi explains: "Like a table that is set and ready to be eaten from."

This means that Moshe was commanded to explain the laws clearly, so that the Children of Israel would have no doubts and would be "ready" to do the *mitzvos* immediately.

Just as in order to maintain healthy and strong bodies our meals must be "ready"—cooked and prepared to be eaten—so, too, in order to maintain healthy, strong Jewish souls, it is necessary for the laws to be "ready," clear and easy for us to understand.

This is also a lesson for all of us to whom the laws have been given:

We must be "ready" at any time to serve Hashem, and not be busy or distracted by other pursuits. This is the sole purpose for which we were created.

When Hashem promised to take the Jewish people out of Egypt, He called them *Tzivosai*, "My soldiers." Also on the day they left Egypt, He called them *Tzivos Hashem*, "Hashem's soldiers."

Every army has a uniform, so that people can identify clearly which army the soldiers belong to. We, too, were given uniforms, which identify us as Hashem's soldiers.

The uniforms are also a sign of readiness:

When a Jewish boy wears *tzitzis*, he demonstrates clearly that he is Hashem's soldier and that he is "ready" to carry out Hashem's instructions.

A Jewish girl, too, has a special way of making it clear that she is a Jewish girl, ready to serve Hashem. She does so by wearing modest clothing suitable for a Jewish girl, Hashem's princess.

(Based on Likkutei Sichos, vol. 21 p. 310)

תרומה
TERUMA

THE ACT OF GIVING IS
MOST REWARDING

This week's *parshah* relates Hashem's instructions on how to build the *Mishkan* and its vessels—the *Aron*, the *Menorah*, the *Mizbeiach* and the *Shulchan*. The Children of Israel were commanded to give donations for this purpose. These donations were called "*terumah.*"

The verse that contains this directive states: וְיִקְחוּ לִי תְּרוּמָה ("they shall take to me *terumah*"). This is difficult to understand because, seemingly, it would be more correct to write: "they shall give *terumah*"?

The *Zohar* explains that when one gave a donation to the *Mishkan*, one became connected to Hashem. Thus, the statement "take (to) Me" makes sense because the giver of the donation is, in effect, taking Hashem unto himself, by connecting with Him.

The same applies when one studies Torah and when one does a mitzvah, such as giving *tzedakah*. This is actually hinted at in the word תְּרוּמָה, which is a combination of the letters that spell out the word תּוֹרָה plus the letter מ (*mem*). The numerical value of *mem* is forty—alluding to the Torah that was given in forty days (Moshe remained on Mt. Sinai for forty days to receive the two tablets).

When studying Torah, one spends time and energy which could have been used for other important things or for personal pleasure. When giving a donation, too, one may have used that hard-earned money for personal things.

This is why Hashem told Moshe to tell the Children of Israel that they should "take" *terumah*. "Take"—because by studying Torah or by giving *tzedakah*, one is actually "taking" and gaining.

In addition, it may be true that giving *tzedakah*, studying Torah and doing *mitzvos* can be expensive or tiring, but the result is that one earns the greatest reward one can possibly receive: a connection with Hashem. We "take" Hashem into our lives.

(Based on Likkutei Sichos, vol. 16 p. 295; Maamar Veyikchu Li Terumah 5725)

תצוה

TETZAVEH

MOSHE'S PRESENCE IN
THIS WEEK'S PARSHAH

The 7th of Adar is the *yahrzeit* of Moshe Rabbeinu. This day occurs during the week of *Parshas Tetzaveh* (or shortly before it), and is indicated in this week's *parshah* as follows: This week's *parshah* is the only *parshah* in all the three books of *Shemos*, *Vayikra* and *Bamidbar* in which Moshe's name is not mentioned.

On a superficial reading, the fact that Moshe's name is missing is a sign that Moshe's physical presence is gone.

The *Zohar*, however, explains that the *spirit* of the *tzaddik*— his faith, his love and fear of Hashem, which filled his entire life—continues to exist in this world after the *tzaddik* passes away, even more than during his physical lifetime.

This being the case, we need to understand why Moshe's name is missing. Although we can no longer see Moshe's physical body, his soul, which is far more important than his body, continues to exist in our midst! According to the *Zohar*, there must be another reason why Moshe's name is not mentioned in this week's *parshah*.

The answer lies in the first verse of the *parshah*: "*You* shall command the Children of Israel." The word "You," obviously refers to Moshe. On a deeper level, it refers to him, not merely to his name, but to his entire being—"You." Indeed, in the entire *parshah*, Hashem speaks directly to Moshe, without mentioning his name.

For his own sake, a person does not even require a name. The name is not connected to any part of a person. Usually, the name is needed merely for others who wish to communicate with the person—they call him or her by name. Alternatively, it is used when we speak about someone in the absence of the person.

In our *parshah*, even though Moshe's *name* is not mentioned, his essence is present and all pervasive.

(Based on Likkutei Sichos, vol. 26 p. 205)

UNITY MAKES US PERFECT

This week's *parshah* begins with the mitzvah of *Machatzis Hashekel*—the half-shekel that was given annually by all the Children of Israel, to pay for the daily *korbonos*.

One of the unusual things about this mitzvah is the fact that everyone is commanded to give exactly half a *shekel*. The rich must give no more. The poor must give no less.

Why should the wealthy—who can afford more—give the same amount as the poor?

In general, the Jewish people are obligated to do the *mitzvos*—especially those performed in the *Beis Hamikdosh*—in the most complete manner. For example: an animal which is to be offered as a sacrifice must be *tamim* (complete, without a blemish), and if it is blemished even slightly it is unfit for the sacrifices. Likewise, in order for their contents to be considered holy, the vessels of the *Beis Hamikdosh* (for flour, oil, wine, and the like) needed to be filled with their *complete* measures prescribed in the Torah.

Why, then, does this commandment specifically, involve an *incomplete*, half *shekel*?

The answer is that the rich man's half-*shekel* together with the poor man's half-*shekel* constitutes one complete *shekel*. When the half is combined with another half, it becomes one complete unit. Thus, the *Machatzis Hashekel is* a complete entity.

One of the beautiful lessons that we can learn from this is that no Jew can consider himself to be "complete" or perfect, unless he or she is prepared to unite with another Jew. We must never look down at somebody else. No one is better than the other. The rich and the poor are considered equal in the eyes of Hashem.

Machatzis Hashekel reminds us that no one is perfect. That is, unless we unite!

(Based on Likkutei Sichos, vol. 31 p. 132;
Sichas Shabbos parshas Vayakhel 5752)

פורים

PURIM

THE SECRET OF
ESTHER'S SUCCESS

I n chapter four of Megillas Esther, Mordechai urges
Queen Esther to beg King Achashverosh to save her
nation—the Jewish people—from Haman's evil decree to
destroy them. Upon receiving Mordechai's message, Esther
agreed to go to the king, but only after all the Jews of
Shushan—including herself—had fasted for three days and
nights.

This is somewhat surprising:

The lives of the entire Jewish people—men, women and
children—were at stake, and Queen Esther was the only
one that could possibly save them. Approaching the king
when not invited was forbidden and punishable by death.
As Esther had not been invited to the king for thirty days,
she was clearly risking her life to meet him. In addition, her
pale complexion as a result of fasting for three days would
only weaken her chance of finding favor in the king's eyes
and saving the Jews. Why wasn't she afraid of losing her
charm by fasting and jeapordizing her possible success?

The answer is that the success of the Jewish people

depends on their connection to Hashem and their ability to receive Hashem's blessing.

Jews in those days were fortunate: Mordechai, their leader, was one of the king's advisors. In addition, he had saved the king's life. Esther—a Jewish woman—was the queen, and she found favor in the king's eyes. Yet, a terrible decree was issued against the Jews.

Esther understood that this evil decree did not come about by chance, but rather, could only have been caused by the sin of the Jews attending the feast of Achashverosh.

Our Sages teach us not to "sit back" and rely on miracles to happen. We must do our utmost to save and protect lives. Indeed, Esther did her part and went to the king as well. Her *priority*, however, was to remove the *cause* of Haman's decree. She was confident that if the Jews fasted and repented for their sin, they would merit Hashem's blessing and her mission to the king would be successful.

(Based on Likkutei Sichos, vol. 6 p. 191)

וַיַּקְהֵל
VAYAKHEL

ALL JEWS ARE NEEDED
FOR THE MISHKAN

I n this week's *parshah*, we read that both men and women participated in the construction and preparation of materials for the *Mishkan*, yet two individuals were singled out: Betzalel, from the Tribe of Yehudah and Oholiav, from the Tribe of Dan.

In many ways, the tribe of Yehudah was considered the leader of all the tribes. All kings from the dynasty of David were descendants of Yehudah. Moshiach will also be a descendant of Yehudah. When the Jews wandered in the desert for 40 years, the tribe of Yehudah always traveled first, leading the way for all the other tribes. Spiritually, they were on a high level.

The Tribe of Dan, on the other hand, was the very last tribe to travel in the desert. Similarly, they were considered to be on the lowest spiritual level of all the tribes.

These two individuals represent two extremely opposite segments of our people. By choosing them, the Torah teaches us that all Jews, regardless of their level of knowledge or observance, have an equal share in Hashem's *Mishkan*.

In fact, even if all the Jews from the tribe of Yehudah had built the *Mishkan* themselves, Hashem would not have rested His holiness there. Hashem would say: if you want Me to dwell in your midst, I need every single Jew, including those who may be on the lowest spiritual level, to be involved and present.

For this reason, the *parshah* does not merely begin with the usual introduction: וַיְדַבֵּר מֹשֶׁה אֶל בְּנֵי יִשְׂרָאֵל ("Moshe spoke to the Children of Israel"), but rather וַיַּקְהֵל מֹשֶׁה אֶת כָּל עֲדַת בְּנֵי יִשְׂרָאֵל ("Moshe gathered the entire congregation of the Children of Israel"). Only after gathering *all* the people together did Moshe speak to them.

(Based on Likkutei Sichos, vol. 1 p. 201. See also above p. 49)

פקודי
PEKUDEI

WE MUST ALWAYS BE READY
FOR THE REDEMPTION

I n this week's *parshah,* we read that on the first day of the first month (*Rosh Chodesh Nissan*), the *Mishkan* was erected. The *Mishkan's* walls were made of cedar wood. Each panel was 10 *amos* (about 20 feet) high.

Where did the Jews get cedar wood in the desert?

Rabbi Tanchuma (quoted in Rashi, *Parshas Terumah*) explains that Yaakov knew that the Children of Israel would be redeemed from Egypt and eventually be required to build a *Mishkan* in the desert. Therefore, when Yaakov moved to Egypt, he planted cedar trees there, so that when the Children of Israel would leave Egypt they would be able to take the cedars along for use in the construction of the *Mishkan.*

Yaakov wanted the Children of Israel to be ready to build the *Mishkan* as soon as they received the instructions to do so. Had he not planted the cedars in advance, it would have taken them a long time to obtain such tall cedars. Moshe would have needed to send messengers from the desert to distant lands to locate them, and the construction of the *Mishkan* would have been delayed.

This teaches us an important lesson: In the same way that our ancestors needed to be ready for the moment of *their* redemption, we, too, need to stand ready for *our* redemption.

Moshiach is ready to come now! We must get ready to greet him!

We do so by conducting ourselves in our own home in a Jewish manner as Hashem would want—by studying more Torah, doing more *mitzvos* and performing more acts of goodness and kindness. This creates an environment of holiness in the home, making it a *Mishkan* in which Hashem can dwell, and making us ready for Moshiach—who will bring our ultimate redemption and rebuild the eternal *Mishkan*, the third Beis Hamikdosh.

(Based on Likkutei Sichos, vol. 22 p. 177, 180; vol. 31 p. 146;
The Rebbe, Sunday, 12 Marcheshvan 5752;
Sefer Hasichos 5752 p. 112)

נ י ס ן
NISSAN

TIME TO PREPARE—
DO WE KNOW THE ANSWERS?

The Shabbos preceding the month of Nissan is *Shabbos Mevorchim Nissan* (the Shabbos when we bless the new month of Nissan). The highlight of this month is the festival of Pesach.

Pesach is a festival that involves a lot of work. Cleaning and preparing one's home for Pesach is no simple task.

Besides assisting their parents in getting the home ready for Pesach, children have their own Pesach preparations as well.

Our Sages teach that when the Jews left Egypt, the young children were the first to acknowledge Hashem's miracles. To commemorate this, each year it is the Jewish children who introduce the Seder night with their Four Questions, the *Ma Nishtana*. Often, children will study these four questions by heart, and recite them at the Seder table.

Now, "by heart" doesn't just mean "from memory," but that the children ask these four questions "with the heart"—that is, "from deep inside the heart."

Year after year, when children ask the same questions, over

and over again, it shouldn't just be a matter of rote. For if that were to be the case, the children would already know the answers from the previous year and wouldn't understand why we are celebrating Pesach all over again this year. Rather, each Pesach should be seen as a new opportunity to discover better answers and reach a deeper understanding of the meaning of Pesach.

And just as children must come prepared with questions, and with a sincere desire to know the answers, parents are expected to tell their children the answers. This is evident in the name of the text that accompanies the Seder tradition—the Haggadah, which comes from the word *vehigadeta*, as in *vehigadeta levincha*, which means "and you shall tell your child."

Therefore, the days of Nissan leading up to Pesach should be seen as an opportunity to double our efforts in preparation for Peasch.

(Based on Likkutei Sichos, vol. 22 p. 179;
Sichos Rosh Chodesh Nissan 5742; 19 Nissan 5749;
Yechidus, 15 Nissan 5737—Tzaddik L'Melech, Issue 4 p. 174)

ספר

ויקרא

BOOK OF

VAYIKRA

ויקרא
VAYIKRA

MOSHE'S HUMILITY—
SEEING GREATNESS IN OTHERS

This week's *parshah* begins with the word וַיִּקְרָא ("He called"). Hashem called to Moshe and told him the laws of the *korbonos*.

The word *Vayikra* ends with an *alef*. In the Torah, however, the *alef*—this time—is written smaller than the other letters, and it looks like this: וַיִּקְרָא. It is called an *alef ze'ira*, a little *alef*. Our Sages teach that this alludes to Moshe's humility. The Torah describes Moshe as the most humble person on earth. And yet, Moshe was also considered to be the greatest man on earth. The Torah tells us that there was never a prophet as great as Moshe.

How can a person be both so great and so humble?

The answer to this lies in the fact that Moshe's humility and greatness are actually connected to each other.

Moshe's humility was different than ordinary humility. Throughout the generations there were many humble people, but none of them were as *great* as Moshe. Yet as long as one is not as great as one can be, one has good reason to be humble.

This is where Moshe's humility was unique. Moshe was fully aware of the fact that he had privileges that no one else had. He spoke to Hashem face to face. He received the Torah directly from Hashem. Hashem made him greater than everyone. Yet, despite his greatness, he remained humble. Moshe knew that his greatness was not to his credit, but was a gift from Hashem. Moshe felt that had others received this gift, they would have been even greater than him. This was Moshe's humility.

Sometimes, even a humble person can get "comfortable" with his humility. He may think: "I know I am not a great man—but neither is my neighbor." This, however, makes his humility questionable.

Moshe's extraordinary humility—which made him truly the greatest man on earth—was his ability to see the greatness of others, and feel humble compared to them.

(Based on Likkutei Sichos, vol. 17 p. 7)

TZAV

EVERY LITTLE DETAIL COUNTS

I n this week's *parshah,* we read about the seven days of *miluim* (inauguration) in which Moshe trained Aaron and his sons to do the *avodah* in the *Mishkan.*

At the end of the *parshah,* the Torah praises Aaron and his sons for following the instructions that they were given precisely and not changing anything.

Throughout the generations, there have been many people who kept all of Hashem's *mitzvos,* although they did not receive their instructions directly from Hashem or Moshe. Would we not expect the same from Aaron and his sons?

The Torah chooses to relate this to us in order to teach the following:

Sometimes, teachers feel satisfied with their student's general conduct or level of observance. Although aware of details which require improvement, they feel that the student will eventually improve on his own. Or perhaps, they intend to tell the student about this later. For now, they think the student is only a "child" or a "beginner."

But from Aaron and his sons' total commitment—*even dur-*

ing their days of training—we learn that a teacher's instructions must be followed and carried out with precision. And even during the early stages of education, *every* little detail counts.

(Based on Sichas Shabbos Parshas Tzav 5725)

פסח
PESACH

THE FIFTH SON

In the *Haggadah*, we read about the four sons: 1) the *chacham*—the wise son, 2) the *rasha*—the wicked son, 3) the *tam*—the simple son, and 4) the *she'eino yodeia lish'ol*—the son who does not even know how to ask.

These sons are very different in both their level of knowledge and observance. Yet they all have something in common. The Torah speaks of all four "sons." All four have some sort of relationship with Hashem.

The wise son obeys Hashem's orders. He asks an intelligent question.

The wicked son is rebellious and goes against Hashem's wishes. Yet he asks a challenging question.

The simple son is not learned. So he asks a simple question.

Even the fourth son, who doesn't express himself at all, *attends* the Seder. We must encourage him and explain things to him.

Unfortunately, there is a "fifth son" as well. No mention is

book of
vayikra

64

made of him because he is not involved with his Judaism at all. Sadly, he does not even attend the Seder.

As we prepare for Pesach, we must remember to reach out to the "fifth sons" and encourage them to join a Seder.

Not a single "fifth son" should be missing from the Seder table!

(Based on the Michtav Kelali, 11 Nissan 5717—

Igros Kodesh, vol. 15 p. 33)

פסח
PESACH

CHAMETZ AND MATZOH:
SPOT THE DIFFERENCE

The two most essential laws of Pesach are the laws of *chametz* and *matzoh*. During Pesach we eat *matzoh* and are forbidden to eat *chametz*. The basic difference between *chametz* and *matzoh* is that *chametz* is bread that rises while *matzoh* remains flat.

Chasidus teaches that our *Yetzer Tov* and *Yetzer Hara* are like *matzoh* and *chametz*. *Chametz* is a symbol of the *Yetzer Hara*, who is haughty, "rises" in arrogance and is very proud of itself. *Matzoh*, on the other hand, is a symbol of the *Yetzer Tov*, who always feels humble in the presence of Hashem. This is why *matzoh* was the first food the Jewish people ate when they first became a nation.

Yet, the difference between *chametz* and *matzoh* is very subtle.

To illustrate this, let us compare the words *chametz* and *matzoh*. *Chametz* is spelled ץ מ ח (*ches, mem, tzaddik*). *Matzoh* is spelled ה צ מ (*mem, tzaddik, hey*). Both words have a *mem*. Both words have a *tzaddik*. The only difference between them is that *matzoh* has a *hey* and *chametz* has a *ches*. Now, when we compare the structure of the *hey* and the *ches* we can see that they are almost identical. Only a tiny gap differentiates the *hey* from the *ches* (ח־ה).

This teaches us a very important lesson:

The difference between arrogance and humility can be very slight, because even a little bit of arrogance is no good. Indeed, even a tiny speck of chametz is forbidden on Pesach.

In addition, the little opening at the top of the *hey* symbolizes an opening to return to Hashem. Arrogance, the *ches*, closes the door on Hashem. Humility creates an opening for Hashem to enter our lives.

(Based on Likkutei Sichos, vol. 1 p. 129; vol. 22 p. 270)

שמיני
SHEMINI

SERVING HASHEM WITH JOY

In this week's *parshah* we are told about how the Children of Israel rejoiced after seeing that their sacrifices were accepted and that the *Shechinah* rested in their midst: וַיַּרְא כָּל הָעָם וַיָּרֹנּוּ ("All the people saw and rejoiced") (9:24).

From this we learn that just serving Hashem—even if we do everything He wants us to do—is not enough. We must do it with joy. Serving Hashem with joy is also a basic principle of the teachings of Chasidus.

Serving Hashem is the sole purpose for which we were created and for which we continue to exist, 24 hours a day, 7 days a week. Indeed, we serve Hashem even as we carry out routine activities such as eating, drinking or sleeping, which provide us with energy to *daven*, study Torah and to do *mitzvos*.

Here are some reasons why this should make us happy:

a) Serving Hashem reminds us that we have a purpose and higher goal in life, and what that purpose is: to serve Hashem. This knowledge should make us feel important and happy.

b) As we can see from the *parshah*, when we serve Hashem, He then dwells in our midst. Imagine how exciting it would be for an ordinary person if a king would honor him with a visit to his home. Certainly we should rejoice when Hashem—the King of all kings—gives us the great privilege to dwell in our midst!

In addition, we know that joy breaks barriers. Happy people find it easier to overcome their difficulties. The same is true with overcoming the hardships of *golus*, which can be achieved through joy.

The letters of the word מָשִׁיחַ (Moshiach) are the same as the letters of the word יִשְׂמַח (he shall rejoice). In the merit of joy alone, we will merit to be redeemed from *golus* with the coming of Moshiach.

(Based on Sichos 18 Nissan 5745, 5751;
Shabbos parshas Ki Seitzei 5748)

תזריע

TAZRIA

WHY ONLY A KOHEN MAY
PROCLAIM WHO IS IMPURE

I n this week's *parshah*, we read that one who is afflicted
with a skin blemish that may be related to *tzaraas*—
which in Biblical days was a punishment for *lashon hara*
(gossip)—must be inspected by a Kohen.

The Kohen must pronounce whether the afflicted person is
considered ritually pure or impure.

To do so, one of two things must be done. Either the Kohen
has to be taught all the details of the laws of *tzaraas*, so that
he would know which blemish renders a person impure
and which does not, or a scholar who knows the laws
should rule and tell the Kohen whether or not to pronounce the person pure or impure. In any instance, however, no one can become ritually pure or impure without the
Kohen's pronouncement.

The ritual impurity of *tzaraas* is the strictest of all the types
of impurities mentioned in the Torah. It is the only impurity
for which the Torah requires the impure person to stay
completely alone outside "the camp of Israel" for seven
days.

To pronounce a fellow Jew as impure in an enormous responsibility. The one making such a decision must do so with the utmost compassion. The Torah didn't trust even a scholar of the highest order or the greatest expert in the laws of *tzaraas* to make this announcement. For this Hashem designated people whose very essence was filled with love for their fellow Jews. He chose the Kohen.

Only a Kohen—who is chosen to bless the people with *love*—can make such a declaration, which will be accepted as the honest truth.

The lesson here is that before one passes any harsh judgement on a fellow Jew he must examine himself in advance to see that he genuinely loves his fellow Jews.

(Based on Likkutei Sichos, vol. 27 p. 88)

מצורע
METZORA

THE CAUSE OF THE PLAGUE
AND ITS REMEDY

In last week's *parshah*, *Tazria*, we read about the affliction of *tzaraas*. *Tzaraas* was a punishment for lashon hara (gossip)—even if the content of what one says is true, the very fact that one is speaking negatively about another person is considered a sin—and the affected person was known as a *metzora*.

In this week's *parshah*, we read about how the *metzora* was purified. This process was not a simple one—the *metzora* was required to sit in complete seclusion outside the "camp of Israel" for seven days.

Although we are no longer punished for the sin of *lashon hara* in this manner, the sin itself is, unfortunately, still very common. Thus, it is important for us to try and find the relevance of this *parshah* and what it relates about the affliction of *tzaraas*, to our times.

The word *metzora* (מְצוֹרָע) is a combination of three words—*motzi (shem) ra* (מוֹצִיא שֵׁם רַע), meaning "one who speaks ill of another (when what he says is false)." For this reason, only a Kohen—one who must embody and exemplify true loving kindness towards his fellow Jew—has the right to declare a Jew ritually impure. This is because declaring someone else a *metzora*, if done by one whose love for his fellow Jew is not entirely pure and true, is itself a form of *motzi shem ra*, and is both false and unkind.

Thus, our first responsibility towards others is to act with loving kindness. If we find fault with another Jew this is a reflection of our own faults and should be a reminder to us to rectify our flaws.

The Midrash compares *golus* to *tzaraas*. The cause of *golus* was baseless hatred. True *Ahavas Yisroel* nullifies the cause of *golus*, and thus brings about the immediate and complete redemption with the coming of Moshiach.

(Based on Likkutei Sichos, vol. 27 p. 91. See also above p. 71)

אחרי
ACHAREI

WHAT HAPPENS
THE DAY AFTER?

This week's *parshah*, *Acharei*, discusses the laws of the *Avodah* of the *Kohen Godol* on Yom Kippur.

The name of the the *parshah*, *Acharei*, which means "after," teaches us an important lesson:

Even after experiencing great spiritual heights associated with the *Avodah* of the holy day of Yom Kippur, one should not be satisfied with this achievement and rest. Instead, one should be concerned with "*Acharei*"—what still needs to be immediately accomplished.

The *Avodah* of the *Kohen Godol*—discussed in the first part of the *parshah*—brought the holiest man, to the holiest place on earth, on the holiest day of the year: the *Kohen Godol* in the *Kodesh Hakodoshim* (the Holy of Holies), which was the holiest part of the *Beis Hamikdosh,* on Yom Kippur.

Nevertheless, the *parshah* does not continue discussing lofty, spiritual matters. Instead, it continues with the laws of forbidden marriages, warning us not to follow the ways of the land of Egypt.

Furthermore, the beginning of the *parshah* is read on Yom Kippur after *Shacharis*, and its conclusion is read later in the day, during the *Minchah* prayer.

Now, Yom Kippur is the holiest day of the year. We fast and pray all day long, and are compared to angels who have no sins. It seems strange that after reading about the *Avodah* of the *Kohen Godol*, we should later read the laws concerning forbidden marriages and not following the ways of Egypt!

This teaches us the valuable lesson of never being complacent and lowering our guard. Even if we have reached the peak of holiness, we must not be content. There is more to do. The ultimate test is *Acharei*—what we do next.

(Based on Sichas Motzaei Shabbos parshas Acharei 5738)

pearls for the
shabbos table

קדושים
KEDOSHIM

TWO LOVES

In this week's *parshah* (19:18), we learn about the mitzvah of *Ahavas Yisroel*. In the very same verse, we are also commanded not to take revenge or to bear a grudge against another Jew.

An example of revenge: Moshe needs a pencil. He asks Shlomo, "Can I borrow your pencil?" Shlomo says: "no!" The next day, Shlomo asks Moshe, "Can I borrow your ruler?" Moshe says, "I'm not going to loan you my ruler, just like you did not loan me your pencil!"

An example of a grudge: Rachel needs a pencil. She asks Leah, "Can I borrow your pencil?" Leah says, "No!" The next day, Leah asks Rachel, "Can I borrow your ruler?" Rachel says, "Here's the ruler. I am not like you." Rachel is not taking any revenge, but she has not forgotten that Leah did not loan her the pencil. She is wrong for keeping a grudge in her heart.

These are ways of fulfilling the mitzvah of *Ahavas Yisroel* by not treating others in a manner that we do not like to be treated ourselves.

Ahavas Yisroel is a major principle, which entails many, many details. For example: inviting guests, visiting the sick, helping a *choson* and *kallah* with their expenses and rejoicing at their *simchah*, are all deeds of *Ahavas Yisroel*.

The following insights from the teachings of Chasidus give us a glimpse into the true meaning of *Ahavas Yisroel*:

1) The people of Israel are the children of Hashem (*Devarim* 14:1). One's love of a fellow Jew is an indication that one loves Hashem. For when one loves the father, one loves his children.

2) Every Jew has a *neshamah*, which is part of Hashem. We must love every Jew because of the G-dliness that is inherent in him. Thus, love for a fellow Jew is love of Hashem.

3) Hashem—whom we love—loves every Jew, as it is written, "'I have loved you,' says Hashem" (*Malachi* 1:2). It follows that *Ahavas Yisroel* is superior to the love of Hashem—for you love whom your Beloved loves. *Ahavas Yisroel* contains within it *Ahavas Hashem*, as well as actually loving a fellow Jew.

These insights help us understand how it is possible, why it is so necessary, and how great it is, to love every single Jew.

(Based on Likkutei Sichos, vol. 17 p. 216-218; vol. 2 p. 499; Hayom Yom 28 Nissan, 24 Menachem Av; Kuntres Ahavas Yisroel pp. 33-34; See also below, p. 117)

אמור
EMOR

SEFIRAH—
MAKING OURSELVES SHINE

I n this week's *parshah*, we learn about the unique mitzvah of *Sefiras HaOmer* ("Counting of the *Omer*"), which
we perform for 49 days between the second night of
Pesach and Shavuos: every night during this period, we
count an additional day. This period is known as "*yemei
hasefirah*" (days of *sefirah*).

When the Jewish people left Egypt, they were told that
Hashem will give them His precious treasure (the Torah) in
seven weeks' time. Looking forward with excitement to
receiving the Torah, they counted each day.

The word סְפִירָה (*sefirah*) does not only mean counting. It
also comes from the word סַפִּיר (*sapphire*)—something that
shines.

At the time of the Exodus from Egypt, the Jews were in a
very low spiritual state, due to many years of slavery under
the Egyptians. When they finally left Egypt, they were not
spiritually ready for the great G-dly revelation during the
Exodus. From the following day on, however, they worked
on self improvement—making themselves "shine"—in
order to be spiritually ready for the giving of the Torah.

Every year, we need to count the days before Shavuos, for we are lucky to be Jewish and that Hashem has given *us* His holy Torah. Counting days reminds us that time is precious. We should not waste time. Every day of life is a special gift from Hashem, and if we use our days properly, we can achieve many great things. With each new day, we should make ourselves shine by learning more Torah and behaving better than the previous day.

The manner of counting teaches us another lesson:

On each day, we count not only the new day, but also the previous days. For example: on the second day, we do not say "Today is the second day of the omer" but rather, "Today is two days of the omer." On the third day, we say "Today is three days," and so on. This is because our good deeds *accumulate*—add up—from day to day. Every day we reach greater heights, so after 49 days of refining ourselves, we are ready to receive the Torah.

(Based on Likkutei Sichos, vol. 3 p. 995;
Hayom Yom 1 & 10 Iyar;
Toras Menachem 5742, vol. 3 p. 1215-1217;
Sichas Lag B'omer 5717;
Sefer Hasichos 5747, vol. 2 p. 391-392)

ל"ג בעומר
LAG B'OMER

AS ONE MAN WITH ONE HEART

The days of *Sefiras HaOmer*, generally, are days of prepa-ration for *Matan Torah*, the Giving of the Torah, which we celebrate on Shavuos.

An essential part of these preparations is to bring more unity to the Jewish People. In the *Haggadah* of Pesach we thank Hashem by saying: אִלּוּ קֵרְבָנוּ לִפְנֵי הַר סִינַי וְלֹא נָתַן לָנוּ אֶת הַתּוֹרָה דַּיֵּנוּ ("Had He brought us to Mount Sinai and not given us the Torah, it would have been enough for us").

This statement implies that just being at Sinai, even before receiving the Torah, was considered a great achievement.

This is because when the Jewish people arrived at Sinai they were united "as one man, with one heart." Not only were there no arguments ("as one *man*"), but they loved each other ("with one *heart*"). The Midrash explains that this is why Hashem decided to give the Torah at that moment.

We, too, prepare for Shavuos and receiving the Torah again, by strengthening our unity and love for our fellow Jew.

book of
vayikra

80

Lag B'omer (the 33rd day of the Omer) is a very joyous day. On this day, the students of the great *tanna* Rabbi Akiva stopped dying. They had been dying from a unique plague because they did not respect each other. *Lag B'omer*—the day this plague stopped, teaches us the importance of *Ahavas Yisroel*.

Another lesson in *Ahavas Yisroel*:

Lag B'omer is the *yahrzeit* of the great *tzaddik*, Rabbi Shimon bar Yochai, known as "Rashbi"—one of the surviving students of Rabbi Akiva.

Both Rabbi Akiva and Rashbi are known for *Ahavas Yisroel*. Rabbi Akiva taught: "Love your friend as you love yourself—this is a great principle in the Torah." Likewise, Rashbi taught us how to go out of our way to help others.

As we approach Shavuos, and celebrate Lag B'omer, we are doubly reminded to prepare for receiving the Torah by improving our *Ahavas Yisroel*.

(Based on Likkutei Sichos, vol. 27 p. 298; vol. 28 p. 7, 233, 241; vol. 32 p. 152 & 262)

בהר
BEHAR

PRIDE—
FUNDAMENTAL TO JUDAISM

This week's *parshah*—which opens with the mitzvah of *Shemittah*—begins with the words וַיְדַבֵּר ה׳ אֶל מֹשֶׁה בְּהַר סִינַי ("Hashem spoke to Moshe at Mount Sinai"). Hence the name of the *parshah* is *Behar* ("On the mountain").

Rashi points out that the intention of the words is to teach us that just as *Shemittah* was given at Sinai, all the *mitzvos* were given at Sinai. In fact, *Pirkei Avos* states that, מֹשֶׁה קִבֵּל תּוֹרָה מִסִּינַי ("Moshe received the Torah from Sinai"): The entire Torah was given to Moshe at Sinai.

What is the importance of stressing that the Torah was given at Mt. Sinai?

The Talmud tells us that when Hashem wanted to give the Torah, a number of tall mountains wished that Hashem give the Torah on them. Each mountain boasted about its height and greatness. But Hashem chose Sinai, the smallest and humblest of all those mountains.

This teaches us the valuable lesson of the importance of humility. We should be humble like Sinai.

However, if this is the only lesson of Sinai, then Hashem should not have given the Torah on any mountain at all! We can appreciate that Mt. Sinai is *smaller* than the other *moun-*

tains, but at the end of the day, it remains a mountain, which means it stands higher than the desert around it, and thereby symbolizes pride. If Hashem wanted to teach us humility, He should have given the Torah in a *valley*!

The lesson of Sinai is twofold: one needs to be humble, for Hashem is "uncomfortable" among the *arrogant*, and humility is essential for Torah study.

However, one also needs to be proud, for pride is a basic element in our service to Hashem. Indeed, the first paragraph of the *Shulchan Aruch* speaks about the importance of pride in the context of serving Hashem. Sometimes, other people may laugh at us when we do a mitzvah. If we lack pride, we may not do it. But if we take pride in doing *mitzvos*, we will never be embarrassed or discouraged from doing them.

This kind of pride does not stem from arrogance, but rather from a determination to carry out Hashem's will. It works well with humility: We can be humble—like Mount Sinai—and look at others as better than we are. At the same time, we should be firm and stand firm like a mountain when facing obstacles in serving Hashem.

This is also why the Torah does not merely tell us that Hashem spoke to Moshe at *Sinai*, but rather, that He spoke to him on *Mount Sinai*.

(Based on Likkutei Sichos, vol. 1 p. 276)

בחוקותי
BECHUKOSAI

ENGRAVING THE TORAH
INTO OUR BEING

I n this week's *parshah*, Hashem's promises us that He will give us many blessings אִם בְּחֻקֹּתַי תֵּלֵכוּ ("If you will follow My laws"), וְאֶת מִצְוֹתַי תִּשְׁמְרוּ ("and if you will keep My commandments").

Rashi explains that אִם בְּחֻקֹּתַי תֵּלֵכוּ refers specifically to Torah study. Hashem is requesting שֶׁתִּהְיוּ עֲמֵלִים בַּתּוֹרָה "that you should work hard in the study of Torah."

How is Rashi's explanation, that the study of Torah must be with hard work and diligence, indicated in the words of אִם בְּחֻקֹּתַי תֵּלֵכוּ?

The answer lies in a deeper explanation of the word בְּחֻקֹּתַי as interpreted in the teachings of Chasidus.

The word בְּחֻקֹּתַי (*bechukosai*), which comes from the word חֻקָּה (*chukah*)—which means "law"—is related to the word חֲקִיקָה (*chakikah*), which means an engraving.

Why is the study of Torah described here as an "engraving"?

There are two types of letters: written letters and engraved letters. Written letters do not come from the parchment or paper upon which they are written. The letters are written with ink and after they are written they can still be erased. Engraved letters, however, are part of the stone in which they are engraved. The letters are not an entity onto themselves; their entire being is the stone itself.

In the Torah, there are both categories as well. The letters in a *Sefer Torah* are written. But originally when the Torah was given, it was given as tablets of stone in which the commandments were engraved through and through.

The phrase אִם בְּחֻקֹּתַי תֵּלֵכוּ teaches us that we must study Torah thoroughly, so that Torah and its lessons become engraved in our mind and inseparable from it, just as engraved letters are inseparable from the stone in which they are engraved.

The words of the Torah should permeate and affect our entire being, to the extent that it becomes our nature to follow the way of the Torah, without having to be told or reminded. This can only be achieved through hard work and diligence.

(Based on Sefer Hasichos 5749, vol. 2 p. 466 & p. 473.
See also Likkutei Sichos, vol. 3 p. 1013)

ספר
במדבר

BOOK OF
BAMIDBAR

במדבר
BAMIDBAR

THE TORAH AND THE DESERT

This week's *parshah*, *Bamidbar*, is the first portion of the fourth Chumash, the Book of *Bamidbar*. The Shabbos when this *parshah* is read usually precedes the festival of Shavuos. The *parshah* of *Bamidbar* is a preparation for the holiday of Shavuos, which commemorates the receiving of the Torah by the Jewish people.

But what is the connection between *Bamidbar* and the receiving of the Torah?

Bamidbar means "in the desert." The Torah was given to the Jewish people in the desert—but this was quite specific and not a coincidence: Hashem chose to give the Torah to the Jews in the desert for many reasons, some of which can be learned from the ways in which the Torah and the desert are connected. Here are a few examples:

1) A desert is an abandoned, empty space that has no designated owner. It belongs to everyone and is a free place for all. Similarly, the Torah is not the exclusive property of an elite group of individuals. It is the inheritance of every Jew, which is itself an indication of the fact that every Jew has the ability to learn and study the Torah. By the same token,

it is important that we recognize that the Torah is relevant to us as Jews wherever we may find ourselves: at home, at work, or on vacation, and that every day of our lives should be imbued with the study of Torah.

2) The desert is a place that is devoid of life. There is no water in a desert and little can grow in its space. The Torah was given in this place to teach us that it remains our obligation even if we are "as poor as a desert."

3) For all the reasons listed above, the desert is a place free of distractions. The Torah was given to the Jews in this space to teach us that we must not let anything distract us from the Torah—that our devotion to the study of Torah should at all times resemble the devotion of the Jews in the desert who had no distractions to keep them from studying the Torah.

4) The Torah was given to us in the desert—a lifeless, dangerous place—to teach us that Torah gives us the power to transcend all obstacles that may arise, and to transform even a desert into a hub of life, in the most profound sense of the word, that is, a life informed by the Torah.

(Based on Likkutei Sichos, vol. 8 p. 236; vol. 28 p. 22)

שבועות
SHAVUOS

THE DAY THE PHYSICAL REALM
MERGED WITH HASHEM

The Talmud tells us that there are different views among our Sages as to whether or not one is obligated to eat on the festivals. But there is one festival when all the Sages agree that there is an obligation to eat: Shavuos.

We celebrate the festivals in commemoration of various events that happened to the Jewish people: Pesach—the Exodus, Shavuos—the Giving of the Torah, and Sukkos—the protection of the Children of Israel in the Desert.

This is puzzling: Pesach and Sukkos both symbolize our enjoyment of a *physical* salvation. Yet, not all our Sages were convinced that an obligation exists to celebrate these festivals through the physical pleasure of eating.

Shavuos is when the Jewish people witnessed the revelation of Hashem on Mt. Sinai and had their greatest *spiritual* experience ever. Yet, here, all the Sages agree that *physical* pleasure is obligatory!

To understand this we must explain the significance of *Matan Torah*:

The Torah existed even before it was given at Mt. Sinai. The

Talmud tells us that the Patriarchs studied Torah, as did our ancestors even during the slavery in Egypt. So why do we celebrate Shavuos altogether?

The explanation is that the Torah itself may have been studied before *Matan Torah*, but it did not elevate the world around it. Even the Patriarchs did not have the ability to transform worldly matter into holiness.

Until the Revelation at Mt. Sinai, the Torah and the world remained two separate domains. Hashem, who created the physical and the spiritual realms, had "decreed" that there be no border crossing between the two. Shavuos is the day on which Hashem made it possible for the physical world to become holy.

While Pesach and Sukkos commemorate pre-*Matan Torah* events, to celebrate Shavuos merely in a spiritual manner would defeat its purpose.

This is why we are obligated to celebrate Shavuos by eating—by enjoying physical pleasure with spiritual meaning and significance.

(Based on Likkutei Sichos, vol. 23 p. 27;
Sefer Hasichos 5751, vol. 2 p. 563)

NASO

THE PRIESTLY BENEDICTION—
WHY NOW?

I n this week's *parshah*, we read the commandment to the *Kohanim* to bless the people, on Hashem's behalf, with the threefold blessing: *Yevarechecha*, *Yaeir*, and *Yisa*.

Following these blessings, Hashem says: "They shall place My name upon the Children of Israel, and I will bless them."

According to the first interpretation mentioned in Rashi, this means that when the *Kohanim* bless the people with the Holy name of Hashem, Hashem joins in and blesses the people Himself.

The fact that we read these blessings during the same week in which the festival of Shavuos takes place—when Jews take it upon themselves to study Torah and practice its *mitzvos*—is no coincidence.

The Torah is teaching us that by keeping the Holy Torah, we receive Hashem's blessings:

Yevarechecha—Hashem blesses us and protects us.

Yaeir—Hashem shines his face towards us and makes us favorable, in the eyes of other nations.

Yisa—Hashem forgives us for everything that should not have happened and grants us true peace.

And when the *Kohanim* mention Hashem's name in these blessings, Hashem not only approves, but gives additional blessings of His own.

(Based on Sichas Rosh Chodesh Sivan 5741;
Sefer Hasichos 5751, vol. 1 p. 42)

בהעלותך
BEHA'ALOSECHA

BRINGING EVERY JEW
CLOSER TO HASHEM

This week's *parshah* begins with the instructions to Aaron on how to light the *Menorah*. The name of the *parshah* is *Beha'alosecha*, which means: "when you (Aaron) will make (the flames of the *Menorah*) rise."

However, a more appropriate word for "lighting" is *hadlakah*. Why does the Torah not say simply *behadlikcha*, which means: "when you will light"?

Rashi mentions two explanations for this: a) *Beha'alosecha* comes from the word *"aliya,"* which means to "go up." This teaches us that the Kohen must not only light the flame, but assure that the flame "rises" and continues burning by itself after he lights it. b) *Beha'alosecha* teaches us that to light the *Menorah*, Aaron walked up special steps in front of the *Menorah*.

The fact that Rashi mentions both explanations must mean that they are connected.

The Torah, in the *sefer* of Mishlei (20:27) compares the soul of man to a flame, and the prophet Zechariah (4:2) compares the souls of the Jewish people to the *Menorah*.

This is the deeper meaning of Aaron the Kohen lighting the *Menorah*: he lit up the souls (flames) of the Jewish people (the *Menorah*).

Nowadays, all of us must follow in Aaron's ways, and we too can "light the flames of the Menorah." We must make every effort to look at our friends and neighbors in a bright and positive way, and notice only the good in them.

This is *beha'alosecha*: to lift up the souls of the people of Israel and bring them closer to Hashem through the light of the Torah. By teaching them until they serve Hashem on their own, we accomplish the first explanation of the word *beha'alosecha*—like the flames that now burn on their own.

In the second explanation of the word *beha'alosecha*, the Kohen went up the steps in front of the *Menorah*, and stood on a higher level. Similarly, when we elevate others, we too are elevated in the process.

Now we can see the connection between the two explanations in the word *beha'alosecha*.

Even little children can fulfill this mission. When we recite the blessings before and after food, when we say *Modeh Ani* immediately upon awakening and *Shema* before going to bed, we bring light into our home. As a result, we influence our parents, brothers and sisters to do the same.

(Based on Likkutei Sichos, vol. 2 p. 316;
Sefer Hasichos 5748, vol. 2 p. 486; 5749 vol. 2 p. 527;
Sichas 13 Sivan 5740. See also above p. 33)

שלח
SHELACH

MODEH ANI—IMMEDIATELY
UPON AWAKENING

In this week's *parshah*, we read about the mitzvah of *challah*, separating the first portion from a batch of dough, as the verse says: "מֵרֵאשִׁית עֲרִיסֹתֵיכֶם תִּתְּנוּ לַה' תְּרוּמָה Of the first of your dough you shall give a portion (*challah*) to Hashem." During the times of the *Beis Hamikdosh*, this portion of bread was given to the Kohen. Nowadays, the dough is simply set aside and burnt. Nevertheless, the lessons of this mitzvah still apply today.

The word the Torah uses for "dough" is "*arisa*," which can also be translated to mean "bed." Thus, the original verse can also be translated as: "Of the first of your beds you shall give a portion to Hashem."

As such, the verse can be understood as a mitzvah to give the first "portion" of our day to Hashem: to acknowledge Him the moment we awake. For the manner in which we begin our day, affects the entire day. Indeed in the *Modeh Ani* prayer we accept Hashem as the "living and eternal King." What we are saying is that Hashem is in charge, and we will follow his orders all day long.

Furthermore, according to Torah law, we are required to

thank Hashem for every pleasure we have, and, appreciating kindness at the very first opportunity, is basic protocol among all of humanity. For this reason, the *Modeh Ani*, which thanks Hashem for restoring life, is recited upon our beds, immediately upon awakening—even prior to the washing of the hands. This is also why our Rabbis did not put Hashems name in the *Modeh Ani*.

Chasidus offers another perspective on the *Modeh Ani*: The reason it is recited even before the washing of one's hands is precisely to emphasize that nothing—not even impurity—can defile the "*Modeh Ani* of a Jew," that is, one's acknowledgment of Hashem. The person's essence, the *neshamah*, remains intact despite any external impurities.

(Based on Likkutei Sichos, vol. 8 p. 308;
Kuntres Inyana Shel Toras Hachasidus, 10-11;
Hayom Yom 11 Shevat;
Sefer Hasichos 5751, vol. 2 p. 812. See also above p. 13)

קרח
KORACH

ONE WHO BELIEVES IN HASHEM BELIEVES IN MOSHE

In this week's *parshah*, we read about Moshe Rabbeinu's cousin, Korach, and his rebellion against Moshe.

Korach was unhappy with Moshe's leadership and said to him: "You appointed yourself as the leader of the Jewish people and your brother, Aaron, as the *Kohen Godol*!" Korach persuaded many other Jews to join him in his fight, among whom were 250 heads of courts.

The truth, of course, was that Moshe and Aaron were leaders only because Hashem had appointed them. Indeed, they were both very humble people.

According to Jewish law, a student is obligated to show respect to his Torah teacher. If this is true concerning teachers and students who are bound only through their minds, all the more so regarding Moshe, who was more than a teacher to the Jewish people. Moshe was called the "Faithful Shepherd" of the Jewish people. This means that besides teaching them Torah, Moshe was like a shepherd who gives his flock everything they need. In fact the Jewish people's entire being—their very existence—was connected to him.

The *Mechilta* (*Shemos* 14:31) says: "One who believes in the 'Faithful Shepherd' (the leader of the people of Israel appointed by Hashem) is considered as though he believes in the word of Hashem. Similarly, one who speaks against the 'Faithful Shepherd' is considered as though he speaks against Hashem!"

Korach was wrong in breaking away from Moshe, Hashem's "Faithful Servant." Therefore, he, his men and their families were punished as though they had rebelled against Hashem Himself.

Throughout the generations, Hashem has provided humble and righteous people as true leaders for the Jewish people, and by following in their ways, we become connected to Hashem.

*(Based on Likkutei Sichos, vol. 4 p. 1049;
Toras Menachem, vol. 22 p. 164)*

חוקת
CHUKAS

ALL OF TORAH IS BEYOND
OUR UNDERSTANDING

This week's *parshah* begins with the laws of *tuma* and *tahara*—impurity and purity. This is known as "ritual purity."

Briefly, "ritual purity" means being spiritually ready to do a mitzvah. It usually requires an act in which someone or something that was previously not fit (spiritually) for a certain mitzvah, becomes ready and suitable for that mitzvah.

For example, *netillas yadayim*, the washing of our hands before we eat bread, is an act of ritual purity. It is not done for cleanliness. In fact, our hands must be perfectly clean *before* we wash for bread. But if we do not perform *netillas yadayim*, our hands would remain "ritually impure"—spiritually unfit to partake of bread.

Another example is immersing new dishes in a *mikveh*. This, too, is not done for hygienic reasons. But as we will read in the *parshah* of *Matos*, vessels made by non-Jews require immersion in a *mikveh* to be fit for Jewish use.

How and why does water make us ritually pure? The Torah

gives us no reason. This law is a *chukah*—a Divine decree—and we need to keep it without questioning it.

So this week's *parshah* begins with the laws of one who comes in contact with the dead and thus becomes ritually impure. In the time of the *Beis Hamikdosh*, he would need to be sprinkled with water mixed with ashes from a *para adumah*, a red heifer, in order to be fit to enter the *Beis Hamikdosh*, or to eat offerings. The Torah gives no explanation for this law.

The *parshah* calls this mitzvah *chukas hatorah* (the law of the Torah), and not merely *chukas haparah* (the law of the heifer), because it teaches us a general rule about the *entire* Torah.

Every mitzvah—even when its reason *is* given—is truly a *chukah* beyond our understanding, for the *entire* Torah is Hashem's infinite wisdom. It is only because of Hashem's kindness that He revealed some of the reasons of Torah's laws, enabling us to understand them. These reasons, however, are not the reason for why we must observe the *mitzvos*. Indeed, we must carry out all of Hashem's orders, even if we cannot understand them. When Moshiach will come we will understand them. Now, we need to do them!

(Based on Likkutei Sichos, vol. 4 p. 1056; Toras Menachem - Sefer Hamaamorim Melukot, vol. 2 p. 164-165. See also above p. 7)

בלק
BALAK

MAH TOVU—
MODESTY IS GOOD

I n this week's *parshah*, we read that Bilam wanted to curse the Jewish people, but ended up blessing and praising them instead.

One of his praises has become part of our daily prayers: מַה טֹּבוּ אֹהָלֶיךָ יַעֲקֹב מִשְׁכְּנֹתֶיךָ יִשְׂרָאֵל ("How good are your tents, Jacob, your dwelling places, Israel").

Our Sages explain that Bilam saw that Jews lived with modesty. Their tents were side by side, yet the entrances to their tents did not face each other. Every family lived with modesty and had their privacy.

One may ask: If the openings to their tents *did* face each other, it would obviously have been a terrible situation. All human beings, not only Jews, have a need for privacy. Why do Jews deserve special praise, more than any other nation, for not prying into each other's personal matters?

The answer is that the Jewish people practice modesty *all* the time and in all aspects of their lives. Many things in life are much finer, greater, and more G-dly, when they are done with *tz'nius*, modesty.

The most well-known is modesty in the way we dress: Torah law requires us to be dressed in a proper and special way that suits Hashem's sons and daughters.

The meaning of modesty, however, is much broader. It means modesty in everything we do—not just in the way we dress.

There is modesty in the way we walk—a Jew should walk in a dignified manner; in the way we talk—a Jew should speak politely, and in a refined manner; in the way we eat and drink—a Jew should eat and drink for the sake of Heaven, in order to have strength to serve Hashem with joy.

Jews are modest always—not only when they want privacy. This is what Bilam, who hated the Jews, understood, and therefore blessed them.

Mah Tovu teaches us that modesty at all times and places, at home ("your dwelling places"), or on vacation ("your tents"—in temporary dwellings), is the good way, the correct way to live. Modesty also has the power to transform the curses of our enemies into blessings.

(Based on Likkutei Sichos, vol. 13 p. 84)

פינחס
PINCHAS

UNCONDITIONAL LOVE—A REMEDY FOR UNCONDITIONAL HATRED

The *parshah* of Pinchas is usually read during the same week as the fast of the 17th of Tammuz.

The fast reminds us of five things which happened on this day. Four of them are connected with the destruction of the *Beis Hamikdosh*, which took place some 2,000 years ago:

1) Moshe Rabbeinu broke the *Luchos* given to him by Hashem in the desert, when he saw that the Jewish people had sinned.

2) Later in history, the Romans broke through the wall surrounding Yerusholayim.

3) The daily sacrifice, the *korbon tomid* (which we read about in this week's Torah portion) was cancelled.

4) The Roman General Apostomus, burned a *Sefer Torah*.

5) He also placed an idol in the *Beis Hamikdosh*.

The Talmud tells us that Hashem allowed the *Beis Hamikdosh* to be destroyed because of baseless hatred (hate for no reason) between Jews.

Unfortunately, this sin is still common in our time, and as a result, we still suffer in this bitter *golus*.

During the week in which we fast for the beginning of the destruction of the *Beis Hamikdosh*, the Torah advises us, in this week's *parshah*, how to resolve the matter.

Hashem granted Pinchas the "covenant of peace"—meaning the rights of priesthood (being a Kohen), which includes the ability to bless the people with peace. Hashem gave the *Kohanim* an additional measure of love for their fellow Jews, as they say in the *berachah* before they give the priestly blessing: לְבָרֵךְ אֶת עַמּוֹ יִשְׂרָאֵל בְּאַהֲבָה ("to bless His people Israel with love").

The lesson from Pinchas is that we should spread peace, love and unity amongst the Jewish people. This will counteract the sins that led to the exile. Indeed, to counteract the baseless hatred that led to the destruction of the *Beis Hamikdosh*, we must exercise unconditional love for our fellow Jews.

(Based on Sefer Hasichos 5748, vol. 2 p. 547; 5750, vol. 2 p. 567.
See also above p. 71, 73)

מטות
MATOS

THE INNER STRENGH OF THE JEW

The *parshah* of Matos is always read during the three week period between the 17th of Tammuz and the 9th of Av—a period which commemorates the destruction of the *Beis Hamikdosh* and the beginning of the *golus*. At this time of year, our yearning for the ultimate redemption is expressed more than throughout the rest of the year.

What is the connection between Matos, *golus*, and the ultimate redemption?

Let us examine the name of the *parshah*, *Matos*.

The *parshah* begins by relating how Moshe addressed the leaders of the *Matos* (the Tribes) of the Children of Israel.

The Tribes of Israel are called *"Shevatim"* or *"Matos."* The roots of these two words are as follows:

Shevet is a soft tree branch, only recently cut, or perhaps, still connected to the tree from which it was nourished.

Mateh is a dry, hard stick, disconnected from the tree and no longer moist with its sap.

book of
bamidbar

106

Like a tree's branches, all Jewish souls stem from their

source in Hashem. "*Shevatim*" alludes to Jews who are attached to Hashem, such as the Jews in the days of the *Beis Hamikdosh*, who came there to serve Hashem and were able to see His presence there. "*Matos*" alludes to Jews who appear to be separated from Hashem, such as the Jews during *golus*, who cannot serve Hashem in the *Beis Hamikdosh*.

However, the purpose of exile is to change our "separateness" from Hashem into something positive. This is accomplished by using our "hardness" in a positive way.

Golus creates opportunities that force us to reveal our deepest strength and to serve Hashem in an uncompromising, "hard" manner, despite all existing obstacles. Were it not for the challenges we face in our *golus* experience, this inner strength would not be discovered.

Like *Matos*—in *golus* we are "separated" from Hashem (we can no longer see Him as we did in the *Beis Hamikdosh*). But like *Matos*—in *golus* we have become stronger—clinging to Hashem firmly, no matter what difficulties arise.

This inner strength of *Matos* will lead to the fulfillment of what the verse in *Tehillim* (110:2) refers to as "*mateh uzcha*" (the staff of your strength), which—as the Midrash explains—refers to Moshiach, who will redeem us from this exile.

(Based on Likkutei Sichos, vol. 28 p. 281)

משעי
MAS'EI

ALWAYS GOING FROM
STRENGTH TO STRENGTH

This week's *parshah* lists all the journeys that the Jewish people travelled during their forty years of wandering in the desert, from the day they left Egypt until they reached the Jordan river, at the border of *Eretz Yisrael*.

Each journey in the desert was followed by a "rest," a place where they camped, and the Torah lists those as well.

Rashi explains that the Torah's description of where the Jews camped helps us recall the many incidents that occurred during those encampments.

Furthermore, the revelation of the Divine Presence in the *Mishkan* took place during their encampments.

Why, then, is the *parshah's* name—*Mas'ei* (Journeys)—and its opening words אֵלֶּה מַסְעֵי בְנֵי יִשְׂרָאֵל ("These are the *journeys* of the Children of Israel"), emphasising the *journey* aspect of their travels?

The answer is that the Torah is teaching us a lesson in our own lives.

The journeys in the desert—in which Jews went from one location to another—also symbolize "spiritual" journeys.

In Egypt, the Jews fell to the lowest level of spiritual impurity. They worshiped idols—like the Egyptians themselves. Yet upon leaving Egypt, they elevated themselves from the G-dlessness of Egypt. Similarly, every Jew, no matter how low his spiritual level may be, has no reason to despair. He has the ability to elevate himself and reach higher levels. This is called a "spiritual journey," and this is the lesson from the name of the *parshah*—*Mas'ei*.

A further thought: the name *Mas'ei* in *plural* means *many* journeys. This teaches us that the Jews made *many* journeys until they arrived at the border of *Eretz Yisrael*.

Similarly, in our own spiritual lives, one spiritual "journey" is insufficient. Jews must always be in "journey" mode, going continuously from strength to strength. For no matter how much good we have achieved, far more is to be accomplished. As Hashem is infinite, there is no limit to the heights we should aspire to reach.

We read this *parshah* on the Shabbos when we bless Menachem Av, (or on Shabbos *Rosh Chodesh Menachem Av*), the month in which our exile began. For just as the journeys in the desert led the Jews to *Eretz Yisrael*, our spiritual journeys nowadays will lead us to the final redemption with Moshiach.

(Based on Toras Menachem 5744, vol. 4 p. 2272)

מטות־מסעי
MATOS-MAS'EI

OUR REDEMPTION—
OUR FATHER'S COMFORT

The *parshios* of *Matos* and *Mas'ei* are usually read together, either on the Shabbos before the start of the month of Av, or on the first Shabbos of Av.

Av is the month during which the *Beis Hamikdosh* was destroyed. The full name of the month is *Menachem Av*. *Menachem* means "comforter" and *Av* means "father"—referring to our Father in Heaven.

Ever since the destruction of the *Beis Hamikdosh*, Av has been a month of particular mourning and yearning for the Jewish people, who turn to Hashem seeking comfort for their sorrows. Similarly, Hashem, who is in *golus* along with His people, is pained by the *golus* and seeks to be comforted by the Jewish people.

If the month of Av was only about Hashem comforting the Jewish people, it would have been more appropriate for its name to be *"Av Menachem"*—Father Comforter (or Father who comforts). Instead, the name *Menachem Av* points to the Jewish people's role as comforters of Hashem. What this means, in practical terms, is that the Jewish people comfort Hashem through an increase in acts that nullify the original cause of *golus* and bring Moshiach closer.

Examples of such acts are *Ahavas* and *Achdus Yisroel*, the study of Torah, especially laws pertaining to the *Beis Hamikdosh*, making or attending a *siyum* of a tractate of the Talmud every day of the nine days between *Rosh Chodesh Av* and *Tisha b'Av*, *tzedakah* and *tefillah*. Through the fulfillment of these and other *mitzvos* the Jewish people comfort Hashem and are in turn comforted by Him.

This theme of dual comforting is contained in both portions *Matos* and *Mas'ei*.

Parshas Matos relates the story of Hashem commanding the Israelites to fight a war against the Midyanim. Hashem refers to this war as "the revenge of the Children of Israel." Yet when Moshe delivers Hashem's message to the Jewish people, he speaks of "the revenge of Hashem," thus emphasizing the fact that our battle is Hashem's battle and vice versa.

Similarly, in *Parshas Mas'ei* we read that "Hashem dwells in the midst of the Children of Israel." From this verse our Sages derive that wherever Jews are exiled, the *Shechinah* is exiled with them. Our exile is Hashem's exile, our pain is His pain, and thus we need to comfort Him as much as we ourselves need to be comforted by Him.

In the same way, the ultimate redemption will be a joyous occasion for the Jewish people and for Hashem.

(Based on Likkutei Sichos, vol. 23 p. 215-223; Sefer Hasichos 5747, vol. 2 p. 494-498; See Likkutei Sichos, vol. 24 p. 335; See also above, p. 73 and pp. 104-105)

ספר

דברים

BOOK OF

DEVARIM

דברים
DEVARIM

EVERY JEW HAS A VISION
OF THE BEIS HAMIKDOSH

The Shabbos on which *Devarim* is read is called *Shabbos Chazon*, because its *Haftarah* begins with the word *Chazon* (vision).

Simply, this refers to the vision of the prophet Yeshayahu, which is described in this *Haftarah*. On a deeper level, the Shabbos itself is called *Chazon*—a "Shabbos of vision."

The righteous Rabbi Levi Yitzchak of Berditchev used to say that on *Shabbos Chazon* every Jew is given a "vision" of the third *Beis Hamikdosh*.

Although we are unaware of this vision, Rabbi Levi Yitzchak's saying holds true, for the source of the *neshamah* of every Jew—which remains in the spiritual world on High and is always connected to Hashem—can see it. Even if we—in this physical world—are unaware of it, every year, on *Shabbos Chazon*, Hashem lets our souls see the third *Beis Hamikdosh* and this affects us deeply.

The purpose of this vision can be explained with the following parable:

Once, a father had an expensive garment made for his

beloved son. The son, however, was reckless, and tore his garment. Giving his son a second chance, the father had another garment sewn for him. But again the son was not careful, and ripped this garment as well. The third time, the father sewed yet another garment, but he did not give it to his son. Instead, from time to time, he would show the garment to his son and would tell him: "When you learn how to behave, I will give you this garment."

Similarly, the Jewish people already had two *Botei Mikdashos*, which were destroyed because of our sins. As soon as the second *Beis Hamikdosh* was destroyed, Hashem prepared the third *Beis Hamikdosh* in the heavens above, ready to descend upon earth.

Every year, on *Shabbos Chazon*, Hashem gives us a "vision" of this *Beis Hamikdosh*, reminding us that He is ready to give it to us, as soon as we are truly ready to receive it.

(Based on Likkutei Sichos, vol. 9 p. 24)

ואתחנן
VAESCHANAN

KNOWING THAT WE ARE ONE
LEADS TO LOVE

This week's *parshah* contains the first paragraph of the *Shema*, which begins with: שְׁמַע יִשְׂרָאֵל ה' אֱלֹקֵינוּ ה' אֶחָד ("Hear O Israel, the L-rd is our G-d, the L-rd is one").

The Talmud tells us what the three letters (*alef, ches* and *dalet*) of the word אֶחָד represent:

The א represents Hashem, because *aluf* means a chief, or master, and Hashem is the Master of the universe. Also, the numeric value of א is 1—one G-d.

The numeric value of the ח and the ד represent the world: The universe consists of seven heavens (all mentioned by name in *Tanach*) and the earth, which adds up to eight, and the numeric value of the ח is 8. The numeric value of ד is 4, representing the 4 directions of the world: north, south, east and west.

In other words: the word אֶחָד means that Hashem is everywhere.

The fact that both Hashem and the world are represented in *one* word indicates that the world could never exist without out Hashem's presence.

No matter which way you point: upward (to the heavens), or downward (to the earth), or whichever direction you may turn—north, south, east or west, Hashem is there. He may be hidden from our view, but He is everywhere.

This is also the reason for the custom to tilt one's head slightly in all six directions, while saying the word אֶחָד during the recitation of the *Shema*.

Understanding how we are always really connected to Hashem brings us to love Him. That is why the paragraph of *V'ahavta*, which is the mitzvah to love Hashem, follows the verse of *Shema*.

The same lesson applies to *Ahavas Yisroel*. Realizing that we are all truly *one* entity leads to a true love for each other. No distance can ever break this love, for no matter where we may go, we always remain one. In fact, distance forces us to think more about each other, revealing an even deeper bond among the Jewish people.

(Based on Sichos 1st night Sukkos 5748;
13 Shevat 5746; 21 Shevat 5748)

עקב
EIKEV

KEEPING THE MITZVOS WHICH
PEOPLE TREAD UPON

This week's *parshah* is called *Eikev*. The simple meaning of the word *eikev* is "because." The Torah tells us that because we obey the *mitzvos*, we will be rewarded—that Hashem will keep His promise of kindness towards us.

In Hebrew, there are other words which mean "because." Why does the Torah choose the word *eikev*?

Rashi explains that *eikev* also means a heel. Certain *mitzvos* are often "stepped upon" with our heels. We treat them lightly. The Torah's message is that we must be vigilant in our observance of these *mitzvos*, too.

Here is a clear lesson for all Jewish children:

The *Yetzer Hara* may suggest to a child that since he is only a child, his conduct does not really matter. It's not so terrible—says the *Yetzer Hara*—if you utter an inappropriate word—perhaps a word whose connotation is the opposite of blessing, or *not* in the spirit of love of (the people of) Israel, or something which is false, G-d forbid. After all— says the *Yetzer Hara*—it's only one word, and you are only a child. It's only a "little" thing, and it's not so important. Do you really think that such little things make a difference to Hashem?

Therefore, the Torah teaches us *eikev tishmeun*—you must obey even when it comes to those *mitzvos* that you may think are insignificant and don't really matter.

In fact, it is these *mitzvos* that are very precious to Hashem. In their merit, Hashem promises us that He "will keep for you the covenant and the kindness that He swore to your fathers." When we keep even these *mitzvos*, which seem trivial, it strengthens the bond between Hashem and us, drawing Hashem's kindness towards us.

(Based on Sichas 16 Menachem Av 5744)

ראה
RE'EIH

THE KING IN THE FIELD

Rosh Chodesh Elul occurs during the week of, or is blessed on, Shabbos *Parshas Re'eih*. Elul is the last month of the year, when we begin our preparations for Rosh Hashanah.

Elul has four letters—אֱלוּל—which, we are taught, stand for אֲנִי לְדוֹדִי וְדוֹדִי לִי ("I am to my beloved, and my beloved is to me").

This famous verse from *Shir Hashirim* (6:3) describes the love between Hashem and the people of Israel. "I am to my beloved" is the love we have for Hashem, and "my beloved is to me" is the love Hashem has for us.

This means that the month of Elul is a special time when Hashem shows extra love for His people.

There is a beautiful parable given by Rabbi Schneur Zalman of Liadi (the Alter Rebbe), which explains the special significance of the month of Elul:

On a certain level, the month of Elul has an advantage over Rosh Hashanah. On Rosh Hashanah, Hashem is like a king sitting on his throne in his palace. It is not easy to get into the palace, which is heavily guarded, and you have to be very lucky to get an invitation. Even those who are privileged to go inside to meet the king face to face are usually overcome with fear and are unable to speak.

On the other hand, during Elul, Hashem is like a friend ("My beloved"), a king who leaves his palace, to visit a field, somewhere out of the city. Out there, even ordinary country people and farmers can meet the king. The king greets *everyone* in a friendly manner and with a smile.

The verse begins with *Ani ledodi* (I am to my beloved), because in Elul it is our task to "greet" Hashem—to accept Him as our King, and to follow His commandments with love.

However, the order of the verse indicates that we must take the first step, and then we receive Hashem's love—as is stated in the second part of the verse, *vedodi li* (my beloved is to me).

Our love for Hashem awakens Hashem's love for us and His blessings to us for the New Year, in the month of Tishrei.

But truthfully, our approach to Hashem is preceded and prompted by His special love for us during Elul. Both this week's *parshah*—Re'eih ("See")—and the Alter Rebbe's parable strengthen our awareness of this love, as if we can "see" it, enabling us to greet Hashem during Elul, through Torah study, prayer, acts of kindness and *teshuvah*.

*(Based on Likkutei Sichos, vol. 2 p. 379;
Sefer Hasichos 5747, vol. 2 p. 547-557)*

שׁוֹפְטִים
SHOFTIM

PLACING JUDGES
AT ALL OUR GATES

This week's *parshah* begins with the mitzvah to appoint judges "at all your gates." This means that in addition to the *Beis Hamikdosh*, every city and every town where at least one hundred and twenty Jewish men live should have a small *Sanhedrin* of twenty-three members, so that its leaders can enforce the law of the Torah. Indeed, this is the way it was in the times of the *Beis Hamikdosh*.

We can learn a special lesson from this Torah law even today.

"Gates" are openings. Our faces have many "gates": the eyes, the ears, the mouth and the nose. They too need "judges."

Our eyes:

What the eye sees has a very powerful effect on our behavior. We must always use good judgement regarding what we choose to see. Is it positive? Is it beneficial? If not, it may be better not to look at it. Our eyes should be used for seeing good and wholesome things.

Our ears:

We are very strongly influenced by what we hear, too. We must exercise our mind's judgement and allow our ears to hear only nice things. We should not allow them to listen to *lashon hara*, for example.

Our mouths:

The mouth needs a judge, too. Before any food or drink enters one's mouth, it must be checked to ensure it is kosher, and a *berachah* needs to be said before it is eaten.

And of course, we must judge the words that come out of our mouths. Hashem did not create the mouth for rude, useless, or unpleasant speech, but for words of Torah, words of wisdom, and positive and friendly talk.

By placing "judges" at all our "gates," we become worthy that Hashem should judge us favorably on the approaching New Year, inscribing and sealing us in the Book of Life, for a happy, healthy, good and sweet new year.

By placing "judges" at all our "gates," we will also merit to fulfill this mitzvah according to its simple meaning, with the coming of Moshiach, who will set up the *Sanhedrin* in the *Beis Hamikdosh*, in Yerusholayim and throughout *Eretz Yisrael*, speedily in our days.

(Based on Likkutei Sichos, vol. 14 p. 277-278; Sichos Rosh Chodesh Elul 5738; 5743; 5744; 5747)

כי תצא
KI SEITZEI

REACHING NEW HEIGHTS
IN YIDDISHKEIT

O ne of the many *mitzvos* in this week's *parshah* is to
build a *maakeh* (guard-rail) on the roof of one's home,
for safety. "When you build a new house, you must make a
maakeh for your roof."

Besides the simple and practical meaning of this mitzvah, it
also serves as a spiritual guide for all those who have built,
purchased, or moved into a new home, or for those who are
beginning a new stage in their lives, such as getting mar-
ried and building a new home amongst the people of Israel.

In order for the *maakeh* to achieve its purpose, it must
stand even higher than the roof—the highest point of the
house.

The roof of a Jewish home symbolizes the highest standard
of Torah observance which we have been accustomed to
thus far.

But when Hashem blesses us with good health and fortune,
and we start a life in a new home, Hashem says "build a
maakeh upon your roof."

Some may feel that they have already reached the highest

standards of *Yiddishkeit* that they are comfortable with—"the roof"—in their old home, and they say, "Enough! We've reached the roof!"

Says Hashem, "Your home is My home! The roof is not too high for Me!" A new home is a new stage in your life—a time to build a *maakeh* and reach new levels, beyond your previous expectations.

At the same time, the Torah emphasizes that it is "your roof" and "your home." We do not need to go for miles, or stretch beyond our limit. Hashem is within our reach, in our own home. We can do it!

The same is true with every new stage in life, such as a new year. Every Rosh Hashanah, we enter new, higher levels. This message is therefore particularly relevant now, during the month of Elul, as we prepare for the New Year.

(Based on Likkutei Sichos, vol. 2 p. 386; vol. 19 p. 210)

כי תבא
KI SAVO

EACH DAY REPRESENTS
A MONTH

This week we mark the 18th of Elul, twelve days before Rosh Hashanah. The 18th of Elul is known as *Chai Elul* (18 is the numeric value of *chai*—"life"—in Hebrew).

Throughout the month of Elul, we hear the sounding of the *shofar*, which reminds us to do *teshuvah*, and the 18th of Elul—*chai*—gives "life" to the *teshuvah* we do during this month.

The 18th of Elul begins a twelve day countdown to the end of the year. Each of these twelve last days represents one of the twelve months of the year—the 18th represents Tishrei, the 19th—Cheshvan, the 20th—Kislev, and so on.

On each of these days, we should look back at each of the past twelve months and review all the things we have thought, said, and done.

We should take stock and list the *mitzvos* we have done well, and those *mitzvos* which require improvement.

But while the past is important, we must also plan ahead. On each of these days, we should look towards the months of the coming year and set goals for ourselves.

For example:

You can take upon yourself to be extra careful to keep all the special *mitzvos* related to the festivals in the month of Tishrei (e.g. the *sukkah* and the *lulav*), to recite blessings on food, or to study Torah daily.

Planning ahead is also not enough. From the 18th of Elul—*Chai Elul*—and onwards, we should at least begin to carry out some of our new resolutions, in real life.

May we all merit to be inscribed and sealed in the book of the righteous; the book of life, good life, long life, and eternal life!

(Based on Likkutei Sichos, vol. 2 p. 389; vol. 19 p. 250)

נצבים
NITZAVIM

HASHEM'S BLESSING
FOR THE NEW YEAR

This Shabbos, the last Shabbos of the year and the Shabbos before Rosh Hashanah, is also the Shabbos before the month of Tishrei.

Usually, on the Shabbos before each month, we bless the new month. Surprisingly, the only month we don't bless is the month of Tishrei—the first month in the Jewish calendar year.

There are a number of reasons for this custom. Chasidus explains that we do not need to bless this month because Hashem blesses it Himself.

Hashem's blessing is written in the opening words of the *parshah*:

אַתֶּם נִצָּבִים הַיּוֹם—"You (the Jewish People) stand this day." "This day" refers to Rosh Hashanah, which is the Day of Judgement (as the *Targum* on *Iyov* 2:1 explains). Yet, says Hashem, you remain *nitzavim*—standing firmly upright, indicating that you will pass this Judgement. Thus, the month of Tishrei is blessed by Hashem.

In truth, even the blessing which we give every *Shabbos*

book of
devarim

128

Mevorchim is not our blessing. It is Hashem's blessing. When Hashem blesses the first month of the year, He potentially blesses the entire year. Hashem's blessing before the New Year empowers us to bless all the other months of the year.

Another point: although Hashem already blessed us on the Shabbos before *last* Rosh Hashanah, when He blesses us today, before *this* Rosh Hashanah, it is a completely new and greater blessing which was *never* given to us before. As Rabbi Schneur Zalman of Liadi (the Alter Rebbe) explains, every year on Rosh Hashanah a new, higher "light" of Hashem which never shined before, enters the world.

Therefore, we too must do the same. With every New Year, we should study more Torah, concentrate more in *davening*, give more *tzedakah*, and do more *mitzvos* and good deeds than ever before.

(Based on Hayom Yom 25 Elul; Likutei Sichos, vol. 29 p. 178;
See also above, p. 125)

pearls for the
shabbos table

ראש השנה
ROSH HASHANAH

THE CORONATION OF THE KING

There are a number of names for and aspects of Rosh Hashanah:

a) *Rosh Hashanah* (Head of the Year—i.e. the Jewish New Year).

b) *Yom Hazikaron* (Day of Remembrance—on this day we are remembered by Hashem).

c) *Yom Teruah* (Day of Sounding the *Shofar*—on this day it is a mitzvah to hear the sound of the *shofar*).

d) *Yom Hadin* (Day of Judgment—on this day everyone is judged by Hashem).

Then there is the inner dimension of Rosh Hashanah, one particularly important in Chasidus: Rosh Hashanah is the anniversary of the creation of man.

Surprisingly, in the Musaf prayer on Rosh Hashanah we say: זֶה הַיּוֹם תְּחִלַּת מַעֲשֶׂיךָ זִכָּרוֹן לְיוֹם רִאשׁוֹן ("This day is the beginning of your work, a remembrance of the first day"). Now, the Torah tells us that man was created only on the sixth day of creation. It follows that the anniversary of the first day of creation is actually not on Rosh Hashanah—but six days earlier, on the 25th of Elul!

We now have two questions: a) Why do we call Rosh

Hashanah "the beginning of your work, a remembrance of the first day"? b) Why don't we celebrate Rosh Hashanah on the day creation began (the 25th of Elul)?

We can answer these questions by understanding the purpose of creation. Everything that existed since the very beginning was created for the purpose of serving Hashem. However, this did not happen until the day of the creation of mankind, when Adam, the first man, recognized the Creator, proclaimed Hashem as King, and called upon all of creation: "Come, let us prostrate ourselves and bow down and kneel before the L-rd our maker." That's when the world truly began to exist for its true purpose.

This concept repeats itself every Rosh Hashanah, when just like Adam, we, too, proclaim that Hashem is our King. True, we do that every day of the year, whenever we recite a blessing and say the words *Elokeinu Melech haolam* (our G-d, King of the universe). But on Rosh Hashanah, Hashem's Kingship is the main theme of all our prayers throughout the entire day. In fact, the first and foremost section added in the Musaf prayers is the section of "*Malchiyos*," which includes the verses that praise Hashem as King.

Our coronation of Hashem as King is the most essential idea of Rosh Hashanah because accepting Hashem's Kingship is the foundation of our service to Him all year long, and accepting Hashem's Kingship on Rosh Hashanah helps us accept His Kingship throughout the entire year.

(Based on Toras Menachem—Sefer Hamaamorim Melukot, vol. 1 p. 29; Likkutei Sichos, vol. 34 p. 322; Michtovim Kelolliim L'Rosh Hashanah of numerous years)

וילך
VAYEILECH

TESHUVAH WITH JOY

When Rosh Hashanah occurs on Monday and Tuesday or Tuesday and Wednesday, the *parshah* of *Vayeilech* is separated from the previous *parshah* and is read on *Shabbos Shuvah*.

Shabbos Shuvah is a combination of two extremes: Shabbos—a day of pleasure and joy—and *teshuvah*, when we repent and regret the wrong we have done in the past. How do these opposites co-exist in a single day?

The answer is that there is really no contradiction at all between the two.

As with all other commandments of the Torah, we are obligated to "serve Hashem with joy" when we fulfill the mitzvah of *teshuvah*. In fact, *teshuvah*—which rectifies all the *mitzvos* we have missed previously—is a cause for great joy. Leaving the control of our *Yetzer Hara* in order to return to Hashem is a cause for the greatest joy.

This idea is indicated in the *parshah* of *Vayeilech*:

Vayeilech means: "He (Moshe Rabbeinu) went." "Going" means leaving one location and making progress towards another location.

Likewise, when one does *teshuvah*, one leaves behind the past and starts on a new path of life.

In the same *parshah*—whose name itself represents *teshuvah*—we find an emphasis on joy, for the Torah relates that Moshe completed writing the Torah which he handed over to the *Kohanim* and the *Leviim*.

This was certainly a cause for great celebration, just like the joy of Simchas Torah, when we complete reading the Torah!

This emphasises the lesson which we have learned above, that the mitzvah of *teshuvah* can and must be fulfilled with joy.

(Based on Sefer Hasichos 5749, vol. 1 p. 4;
See also above p. 68 and p. 125)

האזינו
HA'AZINU

THE HEAVEN AND EARTH
ARE LISTENING!

At the beginning of *Parshas Ha'azinu*, Moshe Rabbeinu says: "Listen, O heavens, and I will speak, and may the earth hear the words of my mouth." Moshe, in his greatness, was addressing the heavens and the earth. But what can a simple Jew learn from these words?

Perhaps what the Torah is teaching us here is that Heaven and Earth really are our witnesses and observe and hear our thoughts, words and deeds. We must never imagine that any good deed a Jew does is too small or too insignificant to be noticed—the Heavens and Earth are our witnesses. And every good deed a Jew does, whether great or small, is important in the eyes of Hashem.

Indeed, even non-living creations are witness to our deeds, and as part of Hashem's great master plan, every creation wants to be included in the fulfillment of Torah and *mitzvos*. In the times of Moshiach, inert creations will also be able to speak. Heaven and Earth and everything in between—from the tiniest pebble to the greatest ocean— will give voice to what they have witnessed. Thus, it is our duty and our privilege to make sure that, wherever we may be, the inspiration of the Torah continues to guide us so that the earth does not one day complain and say "Why did a man walk upon me without speaking words of Torah?" Rather, we should use every opportunity to include our surroundings in the *mitzvos* we fulfill so that when the time comes to bear witness, Heaven and Earth will attest to the *mitzvos* we have done.

(Based on Sichas 26 Elul 5742; Hayom Yom 15 Adar 1;
See also above, p. 31)

שבת שובה
SHABBOS SHUVAH

THE TRUE MEANING OF
TESHUVAH—RETURN

This Shabbos gets its name from the the *Haftarah* read this week, which begins with the words שׁוּבָה יִשְׂרָאֵל ("Return, O Israel"). In addition, this Shabbos is between Rosh Hashanah and Yom Kippur, a period that is called the Ten Days of *Teshuvah*.

Usually, *teshuvah* is translated as "repentance," and *Shuvah* as "repent." Repentance means feeling sorry for something wrong that we have done.

When we have done something wrong to another person that we later regret, we say "I am sorry," and hope that the person will forgive and forget. But this is not the case when we are dealing with sins that have been committed against Hashem. For as we said in the *Musaf* prayer of Rosh Hashanah, "There is no forgetfulness before the throne of Your Glory." Since Hashem does not forget anything, how can Hashem "forgive and forget" when we do *teshuvah*?

The answer to this question can be found in the word *teshuvah*. In truth, *teshuvah* does not merely mean to repent and to be sorry—although both are vital to the *teshuvah* process. *Shuvah* means "return."

We are not strangers to Hashem. We are Hashem's children. A father's love for his child does not depend on how intelligent or well behaved his child is. A father loves his child at all times. Even if a child has misbehaved and decided to leave his father, the father will call out: "Return!"

This is what Hashem does every year. Although He knows everything and He does not forget anything, His love for us is boundless and He does His utmost to bring us back home. This is what *Shabbos Shuvah* is all about: Hashem is welcoming us back home.

Of course, Hashem does not forget what happened in the past. But once we abandon the ways of the past and return to Him, we are no longer remembered for our sins, for as the Rambam (*Hilchos Teshuvah* 2:4) explains, we are now considered completely different human beings.

(Based on Likkutei Sichos, vol. 2 p. 409; vol. 34 p. 64)

סוכות
SUKKOS

UNITED WE EXIST,
UNITED WE GROW

During the festival of Sukkos, we take the Four Kinds mentioned in the Torah—the *lulav*, *esrog*, *hadasim* and *arovos*—and shake them together.

The Midrash tells us that the Four Kinds represent four types of Jews:

The *esrog* (citron), which has a pleasant taste and aroma, is compared to the Jew who studies Torah and performs good deeds.

The *lulav* (date palm branch), which has taste but no aroma, is compared to the Jew who studies Torah but has no good deeds.

The *hadasim* (myrtles), which have a pleasant aroma but no taste, are like those who perform good deeds but do not study Torah.

The *arovos* (willows), which has neither taste nor aroma, are like those who do not study Torah or perform good deeds.

The mitzvah of the Four Kinds, which involves bringing all

these four species together, teaches us that we are all one people, and that we must be united.

Furthermore, each one of these four kinds was chosen because each of these species, individually, represents unity:

The *esrog* grows during all the four seasons of the year. The seasons may differ from one extreme to another, yet they come together in the *esrog*, which survives them all.

The *esrog* does not only *survive* all the different climates. It actually *grows* and matures from season to season. We too, need not only to tolerate one another, but to understand that in order to *grow* in our *Yiddishkeit* and to be better Jews, we need to learn from each other.

The leaves of the *lulav* stick to each other, the leaves of the *hadasim* grow together (each three leaves share one bud), and *arovos* grow in clusters.

This teaches us how important Jewish unity is!

(Based on Likkutei Sichos, vol. 20 p. 257)

וזאת הברכה
VEZOS HABERACHAH

MOSHE'S PASSING AND
SIMCHAS TORAH

The joy of the festival of Sukkos, known as זְמַן שִׂמְחָתֵנוּ (the Season of Our Joy)—which is greater than the joy of all the festivals—reaches its climax on Simchas Torah, the culmination of the festivals of the month of Tishrei.

The *parshah* of *Vezos Haberachah*, which concludes with Moshe Rabbeinu's passing, is read on this day.

How does the reading of such a sad event fit into such a happy occasion?!

The fact that Moshe's passing is read on Simchas Torah teaches us a profound lesson, one that is relevant to Simchas Torah:

During the Exodus and throughout the forty years in the desert, Moshe performed numerous wonders and miracles for the Children of Israel. That generation witnessed the Hand of Hashem and were easily inspired.

After Moshe's passing, these miracles ceased, and a new period of "concealment" began, when Hashem "hides" and no longer shows us open miracles to the same extent. As a result, it became more difficult to have faith.

But this was the challenge that Hashem decided to give His people, and He simultaneously gave them strength to overcome it. Indeed, we read in the *haftarah* of Simchas Torah, that upon Moshe's passing, Hashem blessed his successor, Yehoshua: *"Chazak Ve'ematz"* (Be strong and firm).

Similarly, during the *Yamim Nora'im*, or on happy occasions such as the festive days of Sukkos and Simchas Torah, it is relatively easy to feel spiritually uplifted. On the surface of things, once Simchas Torah is over we will reach a spiritual anti-climax.

However, it is important to keep in mind that Simchas Torah is not only the conclusion of the Torah cycle, but that it marks the beginning of a new one, as well. The joy of Simchas Torah inspires us to continue to serve Hashem with joy throughout the entire year. The challenge lies in the days ahead, when we return to work and all our mundane activities. We must be able to extend the joy all year long.

This is the connection between Moshe's passing and Simchas Torah: both give us extraordinary abilities to overcome the challenges of the spiritual void ahead.

(Based on Toras Menachem, vol. 13 p. 53)

שמחת תורה
SIMCHAS TORAH

CELEBRATING ON
SHEMINI ATZERES

Following Sukkos comes the joyous festival of Shemini Atzeres and Simchas Torah—when we complete reading the very last portion of the Torah and then immediately begin reading from the very beginning all over again.

In honor of this occasion, we take the *Sifrei Torah* out of the Holy Ark and dance with them. There is intense joy at this time, and it attracts all types of Jews, regardless of level of Torah knowledge or observance, because every single Jew is connected to Hashem and therefore connected to the Torah.

Now, why is this celebration held at Shemini Atzeres? Why don't we celebrate our connection to the Torah on Shavuos, the day Hashem gave the Torah to the Jewish people?

One answer is that Shavuos was only the beginning of the process of getting the Torah. Forty days after Shavuos, the Jewish people got the first set of *luchos*, but Moshe smashed those *luchos* when the nation made the Golden Calf. After another forty days during which Moshe prayed to Hashem to forgive His people, Hashem instructed Moshe to prepare a second set of *luchos*, which were only given after yet another forty days had passed. The day Moshe came down from the mountain with the second *luchos* was none other than Yom Kippur.

Each set of *luchos* had its own virtues, but because the second *luchos* were a result of *teshuvah* done by the Children of Israel, they remained whole. In this sense, the culmination of the giving of the Torah was on Yom Kippur.

Truly, the celebration of Simchas Torah is due on Yom Kippur. However, because eating and drinking are forbidden on Yom Kippur, it can't be held on that day itself. Instead, it is held on Shemini Atzeres.

The Torah says that Shemini Atzeres is a time "*lochem*" (for you)—exclusively for the Jewish people—to celebrate with the Creator. Over the seven days of Sukkos, a total of seventy sacrifices were brought in the *Beis Hamikdosh*, representing the seventy nations who all are part of the world that Hashem has created. But on Shemini Atzeres, a special sacrifice in the *Beis Hamikdosh* represented the Jewish people alone. For it is a time when Hashem reinforces the connection made during Tishrei and keeps His precious children close to Him for one more special day. The relationship between Hashem and His people on this day is similar to His relationship with them on Yom Kippur, when the Jewish people return to Hashem and are united with Him. So it's the right time to celebrate!

(Based on Toras Menachem—Sefer Hamaamorim Melukot, vol. 1 pp. 210-211; pp. 216-217; p. 225)

APPENDIX

GLOSSARY
INDEX

GLOSSARY

Achdus Yisroel: Jewish unity.

Ahavas Hashem: Love of G-d.

Ahavas Yisroel: Love of the Jewish people.

Alter Rebbe: (lit. Old Rabbi), Rabbi Schneur Zalman of Liadi (1745-1813).

Amidah: (Lit., "standing.") A section of the prayers which is recited silently and standing at attention, known also as shmoneh esrieh; climax of the prayers.

Amos (sing. Amah): Cubits, measurement of an arms length.

Aron: Ark.

Avinu: Our Patriarch (father).

Avodah: Divine service; services of Korbonos in the Beis Hamikdosh.

Avraham: First of the patriarchs of the Jewish people.

Bas: Daughter.

Beis Hamikdosh: Holy Temple in Jerusalem.

Berachah: Blessing.

B'nei Yisrael: The Children of Israel (the Jewish people).

Bris milah: Circumcision.

Chabad: Acronym for Chochmah, Binah, Daas (wisdom, understanding and knowledge); Lubavitch.

Chai Elul: Eighteenth day of the month of Elul; respective birthdays of Rabbi Yisrael Baal Shem Tov, founder of the Chasidic movement (5458/1698), and Rabbi Schneur Zalman of Liadi, founder of Chabad Chasidism (5505/1745).

Chanukas Habayis: House consecration.

Chasidus: Inner dimension of Torah, taught by Chasidic Rebbes.

Chesed: Kindness.

Choson: Bridegroom.

Chuppah: Wedding canopy.

Davening: Reciting prayers.

Eretz Yisrael: The Land of Israel.

Gematria: Numerical value.

Gemilus chasadim: Deeds of kindness.

Golus: Exile.

Hachnasas orchim: Hospitality; inviting guests into one's home.

Haftarah: Section from the books of the Prophets read in the synagogue following the Torah portion.

Haggadah Shel Pesach: Service of Passover read at the Seder.

Hashem: G-d.

Hodu: A prayer recited in the beginning of the morning prayers.

Kallah: Bride.

Kippah: Head covering worn by Jewish men and boys.

Kohen; Kohanim: Jewish priest(s). During the time of the *Beis Hamikdosh* the priests performed the service there.

Kohen Godol: The High Priest, elevated amongst the Kohanim and performed the Service in the *Beis Hamikdosh* on Yom Kippur. See *Kohen*.

Korbon tamid: The daily sacrifice in the *Beis Hamikdosh*.

Korbonos: Sacrifical offerings.

Kosher: Suitable for use; food that Jews are permitted to eat.

Lashon hara: Speaking ill of another.

Leviim: Members of the tribe of Levi.

Luchos: Tablets given to Moses at Sinai on which were inscribed the Ten Commandments.

Lulav: Date palm branch; one of the four kinds shaken during the festival of Sukkot.

Mah Nishtanah: Four questions asked at the Passover Seder.

Megillas Esther: Book of Esther (read on the holiday of Purim).

Menorah: Candelabra.

Midrash: Commentary to the Torah, authored by the Sages.

Mikveh: Pool of natural water for ritual purification.

Mishkan: Portable sanctuary for G-d, built by the Jewish people after leaving Egypt.

Mitzvah (pl. Mitzvos): Commandment(s).

Mizbeiach: Altar.

Modeh Ani: Prayer of thanks, recited immediately upon awakening.

Moshiach: Redeemer of the Jewish people.

Musaf: Additional Amidah prayer recited on Shabbat, Festivals and Rosh Chodesh.

Neshamah: Soul.

Parshah: Torah portion.

Pasuk: Verse.

Pesach: Festival of Passover.

Pesukei Dezimrah: (Lit., "verses of praise.") Section of the morning prayers between the blessings of Baruch Sheamar and Yishtabach.

Pirkei Avos: Ethics of Our Fathers.

Rabbeinu: Our Teacher.

Rambam: Rabbi Moshe ben Maimon; Maimonides (1135-1204).

Rashi: Rabbi Shlomo Yitzchaki, chief commentator of the Torah and the Talmud (1040-1105).

Rebbe: Teacher, Chasidic Rabbi or leader.

Rosh Chodesh: (Lit., "head of the month.") Beginning of the Jewish month.

Rosh Hashanah: (Lit., "head of the year.") Beginning of the Jewish year.

Sanhedrin: The Jewish High court.

Sarah, Rivkah, Rachel, and Leah: The Matriarchs of the Jewish people.

Seder: Order of home service on the first two nights of Passover.

Sefer Torah: Torah scroll.

Shabbos Bereishis: The Shabbos when we read the first portion of the Torah, called Bereishis.

Shabbos Shuvah: The Shabbos which occurs during the Ten Days of Atonement.

Shalom: Peace.

Shavuos: (Lit., "weeks.") Festival of Pentecost, celebrated seven weeks after Pesach.

Shechinah: Divine Presence.

Shema: Three paragraphs from the Torah which we are commanded to recite every morning and evening, and begins with the words *"Shema Yisroel."*

Shemittah: The Sabbatical Year.

Shofar: Ram's horn blown on Rosh Hashanah.

Shul: Synagogue.

Shulchan: Table.

Shulchan Aruch: Code of Jewish Law.

Simchah: Joy, or joyous occasion, e.g. a wedding.

Simchas Torah: Festival when we complete reading the Torah and celebrate by dancing with the Torah scrolls.

Siyum: Conclusion of a tractate of the Talmud.

Sukkah: Hut of temporary dwelling for the festival of Sukkos.

Sukkos: (sing. Sukkah) Festival of Tabernacles.

Talmud: Extensive explanation of the Oral Law by the Sages.

Tanach: Acronym for Torah (Pentateuch), Neviim (Prophets), Kesuvim (Writings).

Tanna: Sage of the Mishnah.

Tefillah: Prayer.

Teshuvah: Returning to G-d; repentance.

Tishah B'Av: Ninth day of the month of Av; a fast day commemorating the destruction of the Beis Hamikdosh.

Torah: Bible.

Tzaddikim: Righteous men.

Tzaraas: Leprosy.

Tzedakah: Charity.

Tzitzis: Four cornered garment with fringes worn by men and boys.

Yaakov: Third of the Patriarchs of the Jewish people:

Yahrzeit: Anniversary of passing.

Yamim Noraim: Days of Awe; Rosh Hashanah and Yom Kippur.

Yerusholayim: Jerusalem.

Yeshivah: House of Torah Study.

Yetzer Hara: Evil Inclination.

Yetzer Tov: Good Inclination.

Yetzias Mitzrayim: The Exodus from Egypt.

Yiddishkeit: Judaism.

Yitzchak: Second of the Patriarchs of the Jewish people.

Yom Kippur: The Day of Atonement.

Zohar: Holy book containing mystical interpretations of the Torah, written by Rabbi Shimon bar Yochai.

INDEX

pearls for the
shabbos table

הוצאת ספרים

קרני הוד תורה

ליובאוויטש